VANTAGE

SUCCESS WITH BEC

THE NEW BUSINESS ENGLISH CERTIFICATES COURSE

STUDENT'S BOOK

JOHN HUGHES

Summertown Publishing

HEINLE
CENGAGE Learning

Australia • Brazil • Japan • Korea • Mexico • Singapore • Spain • United Kingdom • United States

CONTENTS

1.1   Ways of working

Different ways of working

1 How do you work most effectively? By working ...

- regular hours / flexible hours?
- from home / in an office?
- in a team / on your own?
- for a boss / as your own boss?

Compare your responses with a partner.

2 Match these ways of working 1–8 to definitions A–I. Do you work in any of these ways?

0 freelance
1 teleworking
2 job-sharing
3 shift work
4 part-time
5 temping
6 consultancy
7 flexitime
8 hot-desking

A You work during different parts of the day (eg nights).
B You sell your work or services to a number of different companies.
C You work for different companies for a short time without a permanent contract.
D You work a number of hours per week or month but you decide when you start or finish.
E You don't have a permanent place or office to work from, but you find a place to work when you arrive.
F You work for a company from home via email, phone or the Internet.
G You only work for some of the week (not full-time).
H You do your job for part of the week and another person does it for the other part.
I You aren't employed by a company, but are paid to give specialist advice.

3 Here are some people describing the advantages and disadvantages of different ways of working. Match the nine ways of working in exercise 2 to their comments. Some comments might describe more than one way.

It's great because I'm my own boss, but I still work with lots of different people.

I wish I had my own space. I have to carry everything around in my bag and sometimes there's nowhere to sit.

I like it because it's only for a couple of months and I'm saving up to go round the world.

The only problem is sleeping. Your body never knows if it's night or day!

It can get a bit lonely at times. And I miss my colleagues and all the office gossip.

My children are at school so it lets me spend more time with them.

When one of us wants a week off, the other person does a few extra days so it's fairly flexible.

4 Work in pairs. Think of one more advantage or disadvantage for each way of working in exercise 2.

5 Read about job-sharing. Write these headings into each paragraph.

Get organised   Set your limits
Put pen to paper   Two become one
Open your mind   Plan for disaster
Find the perfect partner   Don't feel guilty

How to job-share

Wouldn't it be nice if the working week finished on Wednesday? With a job-share it can. Here's the essential guide to making it work.

(0) Find the perfect partner

Find someone you like. 'Be prepared to communicate and share credit and blame,' says Carol Savage, the managing director of Flexecutive, a flexible working consultancy.

(1) _____

Bosses should consider requests for flexible working from employees with children under six. So embrace the benefits: 'Twice as much experience, skills, brainpower and energy,' Savage says.

(2) _____

Always discuss the worst-case scenarios. When Margaret Mills, a teacher, lost her job-share partner because of a family illness, a return to full-time work seemed inevitable. 'We had been over-optimistic. I did manage to find someone else who fitted in with me, but I was very lucky.'

(3) _____

Plan the system for handing work over carefully and play to each other's different strengths. Delegate the workload according to each other's particular skills and qualities.

(4) _____

Managers should clarify what they expect in terms of hours, availability and results, and employees should manage their employer's expectations. Sue Osborn, a job-sharer for 21 years, says, 'We're often asked to do five-day weeks. Eventually you just have to say no.'

(5) _____

Agree in writing arrangements for holidays, parental leave, retirement, etc. Everyone should know where they stand from the beginning.

(6) _____

Do not work until 1am at home to make up for not being in the office every day.

(7) _____

Clients may not like having to deal with two people so work closely together. As Savage says: 'A job-share should be like a marriage – one voice, one unit.'

6 How easy would it be for you to job-share? Would your employer or boss think it was a good idea?

Working from home

1 🔄 **1.1 You will hear a woman called Michela talking about working from home.**

1 What does she say is important when working from home?
2 What does she think are some of the advantages and disadvantages of this way of working?

2 🔄 **1.1 Listen again and answer the following.**

1 Complete the notes about Michela's typical day.

> 7.00 – get up, get the kids ready
>
> 8.30
>
> 9.00
>
> 12.00
>
> 14.30

2 How long has she been with her current employer? How long has she been home-working?
3 Is she doing anything different from normal this week?

Present tenses

3 Match the sentences from the listening to the grammar explanations.

Sentences	Explanations
1 'I always get up around seven.'	A a state that started in the past and continues to the present
2 'I've been doing this kind of work for about five years.'	B a routine activity
3 'I've been with the same company since I left school.'	C an activity taking place at or around the time of speaking
4 'I'm going into the office nearly every day this week.'	D an activity that started in the past and continues in the present

4 Name the tenses in exercise 3.

> present continuous   present perfect continuous
> present simple   present perfect simple

Grammar Tip

We don't usually write 'state' verbs such as *be, need, like, have* (for possessions), *love, hate* in the continuous form.

5 Write the verb in brackets in its correct form and complete these tips for working from home.

Working from home

0 Even at home, always *set* (set) yourself a timetable.

1 You _____ (need) to find a quiet place to work, where there are no distractions.

2 If you _____ (communicate) with a client on the phone today rather than face-to-face, it's still important to dress for work as normal.

3 Now that you _____ (escape) from the office, you'll still need peace and quiet at home. Don't answer the door to neighbours or make social calls.

4 Once you _____ (work) from home for a while, you might feel a bit lonely. It might be worth going into the office once or twice a week.

5 After you _____ (be) at the computer for a few hours, remember to take a break – why not leave the house and go for a walk outside?

6 Be strong. When a friend calls and asks you out to lunch, say what you would say in any other job: 'Sorry but I _____ (work) on something at the moment. How about after five instead?'

7 Make sure colleagues and clients can reach you and _____ (answer) the phone as though you are in the office.

A mini-presentation

SPEAKING

Exam Success

In Part Two of the speaking test, the examiner will ask you to give a presentation entitled 'What is important when ...?'

6 Work in pairs. Choose one of the ways of working below and prepare a 'mini-presentation' on the topic for the rest of the class.

A: **WHAT IS IMPORTANT WHEN ...?**

Job-sharing

* Find someone you like.

* Organise and plan how you share the work.

*

*

B: **WHAT IS IMPORTANT WHEN ...?**

Working from home

* Set up an office space in the house.

* Plan your working hours and your breaks.

*

*

1.2 Making contacts

Job responsibilities

1 Tell your partner about your job. Use these expressions and choose the correct preposition.

I work *of / for / about* ...

I'm responsible *for / of / about* ...

I usually report *up / at / to* ...

I specialise *about / in / for* ...

I'm involved *in / of / for* ...

I deal *for / with / of* ...

I'm in charge *for / of / to* ...

2 Think of one person you see and speak to in connection with your work ...

- at least once a day _____
- once every six months _____

Tell your partner about these two people. Explain the connection and what they do.

3 Why is making contacts, or 'networking', an important part of many jobs? Is that true for you?

4 Read the article below about some new networking groups specifically for businesswomen. Choose the best word A, B or C to fill the gaps 1–10.

Life's all about making connections

1 A attending	B going	C meeting
2 A ideas	B sugar	C money
3 A department	B company	C group
4 A work	B charge	C responsible
5 A to	B in	C about
6 A run	B control	C produce
7 A speak	B know	C be
8 A do	B see	C make
9 A socialising	B work	C extra
10 A talk	B win	C success

To you, networking might mean (**1**) _____ a conference or trade fair event to meet new clients or partners. Or it could be the coffee break at work where you share (**2**) _____ with colleagues in other departments. But nowadays networking has become an event in itself.

For example, Pricewaterhouse Coopers offer its female staff a formal networking (**3**) _____ called PwCwomen. With 900 members, it organises events ranging from informal drinks evenings to coaching events. Tina Hallet, who is (**4**) _____ for the group, says that she got involved (**5**) _____ networking because 'I'd got to a reasonably senior level and I wanted to help other people to maximise their potential.'

You don't have to be senior to (**6**) _____ a network though. Vicky Wood and Sally Hopkins had the idea for the City Girls Network when they first moved into London's corporate world and wondered how to get to (**7**) _____ other women. 'We couldn't find anything for people with no experience. So we thought we'd start our own.' From twelve friends meeting regularly, it rapidly grew to 250 members from many different organisations. It's a great way to (**8**) _____ useful contacts and bring in potential business.

Fiona Clutterbuck is co-chair of a network for the bank ABN AMRO. 'Women tend to think of networking as (**9**) _____ and give it low priority.' But given the chance, women will network – as the bank's last 'speed networking' event demonstrated. 'With over 100 women and men, it was a great (**10**) _____. It is amazing how many people you get to meet from different parts of the organisation.'

5 According to the article, where do people network and what are the reasons? Would it be useful for you to join or set up similar networks?

Starting a conversation

6 📀 1.2 Listen to four people starting conversations. In each conversation decide where the speakers are making contact.

Conversation 1: _____
Conversation 2: _____
Conversation 3: _____
Conversation 4: _____

A At a conference
B Over dinner
C In someone's office
D On a training course

7 Match the expressions on the left to the responses on the right.

0 I'd like to introduce you to Marek.
1 Nice to meet you at last.
2 Do you two know each other already?
3 Would you like a coffee?
4 So have you enjoyed this morning?
5 Is this your first time at one of these events?
6 May I join you?
7 You're a colleague of Martin Obach, aren't you?
8 How do you know him?
9 How many children do you have?
10 Have you always lived in Lille?
11 I know your company is looking for a partner on this Thai project.

A Yes, it is. And you?
B Hello, Marek. How do you do?
C Thanks.
D Pleased to meet you too.
E Sure.
F Two. Twins.
G Yes, most of my life.
H Yes. Is that something you might be interested in …?
I Well, we've spoken on the phone a few times.
J Yes, it was very interesting.
K That's right. He works in our Barcelona office.
L We were both at Elcotil together.

8 📀 1.2 Listen and check your answers.

9 Work in pairs. One student says expressions 0–11. The other student closes this book and gives an appropriate response.

10 In conversation 4, the two people start discussing personal topics such as where they live and their family. Would you discuss these topics in your country with business colleagues? What do you think are good topics for networking? Make a list of topics with your partner.

Developing a conversation

11 Work as a class or in large groups. You are at a networking event so stand up and walk around. Meet one person and have the conversation below. At the end, move on to a new person.

greet the other person ▶ introduce yourself ▶ talk about the event ▶ describe your job ▶ talk about where you come from ▶ find a reason for doing business in the future ▶ introduce your partner to someone else ▶ meet another person

Business correspondence

I **Read the correspondence on Evelyn's desk and answer these questions.**

1 Is it all related to her work?
2 Which is formal? What is it about the content and language which tells you this?
3 Which is 'internal communication'? Did anyone else receive it?
4 How is the memo different to the letter and the email? Think about the following:
  • the layout
  • the beginning and the end
  • the paragraphs
5 Find abbreviations which mean the following:
  • telephone number
  • as soon as possible
  • at
  • Subject (or) With reference to

To: **All Staff**
From: **Ray Bonner**
Date: **24th June**
Subject: **Trial of flexitime system**

Further to our previous meeting, we are pleased to be able to confirm that the new flexitime system will come into operation as from 1st August. The system applies to all administrative and office staff. May I remind you that any production staff on the current shift system remain unaffected by these changes.

From: evelyn@larbonner.com

Hi Rona

How are you? I got a note to say you called. Great news that you passed your final exam! I'm sorry that I didn't get back to you but it's been crazy here. The network was down for three days so all our customers were receiving the wrong orders! Anyway, how about meeting for lunch this week? If you can't make it, don't forget the party this weekend. Do you want me to pick you up at 8?

See you soon.

Eve

Lar Bonner

Dear Mr Hynes

RE: Replacement of item 00-A104

With regard to your letter dated 12th June, I am writing to confirm that we can offer you a replacement item and this will be sent out today. I would like to apologise for the delay in dealing with this. Unfortunately, this was due to recent changes to our network. On behalf of Lar Bonner I would like to thank you for your custom. We look forward to working with you again in the future.
Yours sincerely

Evelyn Boer

Customer Services
Tel. 0207 865 849

Eve – Can you call someone called Rona back asap? She passed!

2 Complete this table of phrases for writing emails, letters, notes and memos with the underlined words in Evelyn's correspondence.

	More formal	Less formal
Opening salutation	Dear …	Hi …
Give reason for writing	**(1)** _____	Just a quick note to say …
Refer to previous contact	**(2)** _____ _____ **(3)** _____ _____	Thanks for your email … It was good to see you last week …
Make a suggestion	I would like to suggest that …	**(4)** _____ What about …
Apologise	**(5)** _____ _____ We apologise for any inconvenience caused by …	I'm afraid that … **(6)** _____
Give good news	We are delighted to … **(7)** _____	Great news!
Give bad news	**(8)** _____ We regret to tell you that …	The bad news is …
Request	I would be grateful if you could …	**(9)** _____
Offer help	If you have any further queries / problems, please do not hesitate to contact me …	**(10)** _____ _____
Remind	**(11)** _____	**(12)** _____
Refer to future contact	**(13)** _____ _____ _____ I look forward to meeting you again soon.	**(14)** _____
Closing salutation	Yours faithfully (when the letter begins *Dear Sir / Madam*) **(15)** _____ (when the letter begins *Dear Mr / Ms / Mrs*)	Best regards / wishes All the best

3 You are a manager at Lar Bonner. After a meeting with staff, the company has agreed to extend parental leave for fathers from two weeks to three weeks. Write a memo to all staff.

- Refer to the previous meeting.
- Say when the new system will begin (25th September).
- Remind staff that their managers need one month's notice.

1.3 Speaking Test: Part One

There are three parts to the Speaking Test. In this Exam spotlight you will look at Part One, which lasts for three minutes in total. The examiner will ask questions to both candidates during this time. The questions are quite general at first: about yourself, your studies or career, and about where you come from. Afterwards, he or she may also ask you questions about business topics.

1   **Here are some responses by a candidate to the general questions in this part of the test. They each contain one mistake. Can you correct them?**

0   My name ’s Pierre.

A   Yes, I am thinking English is very important for this kind of work because everyone uses English in business nowadays.

B   Well, it's a business studies degree and I'm interesting in marketing.

C   I from a small town in northern Switzerland.

D   I'd like work in a marketing department so I've started applying for jobs with companies in Switzerland.

E   Actually, I'm just finish my degree at the University of Zurich.

F   Since about six years.

2   **Complete the beginning of a Speaking Test with answers 0–F from exercise 1.**

Examiner	First of all, I'd like to know something about you. What's your name?
Candidate	(1) _____
Examiner	And where are you from?
Candidate	(2) _____
Examiner	Do you work or are you a student?
Candidate	(3) _____
Examiner	OK. So what do you like most about your studies?
Candidate	(4) _____
Examiner	What are your plans for the future?
Candidate	(5) _____
Examiner	Do you think English will be important to you in your career?
Candidate	(6) _____
Examiner	So how long have you been learning English?
Candidate	(7) _____

3   **Work in pairs. Practise a similar conversation between the examiner and the candidate using the questions in exercise 2.**

4 After the general questions, the examiner will ask you about business topics. Here are some typical topics for the conversation.

- Business in your home town or country.
- The importance of English in business.
- The effect of technology on business.
- Present and future changes in working life.
- Training and development in the workplace.
- Ways of selling products or services.

5 🎧 1.3 Listen to part of a Speaking Test. Which two topics in the list does the examiner ask about?

6 🎧 1.3 Listen again. Complete the missing words in this part of the conversation.

Candidate Err, well, (**1**) _____ _____ _____ tourism is quite important to the area and there are many small farms so agriculture also. Zurich, where I study, is more famous of course for banking and financial services.

Examiner How is working life changing in your country?

Candidate Sorry, (**2**) _____ _____ _____ the question, please?

Examiner Yes, how is working life changing in your country?

Candidate (**3**) _____ _____ _____ more and more people are moving to the cities or they are commuting in every day. (**4**) _____ _____ _____, the biggest change has come from technology – but then that's probably true everywhere, not just in my country ...

7 Work in pairs. Prepare one question for each of the six topics in exercise 4. Next, change your partner. In your new pairs, take turns to be the candidate and the examiner. Ask each other your questions and answer them.

EXAM SELF-CHECK

8 When you practise Part One of the Speaking Test, evaluate your own or each other's performance with this checklist.

Did you ...	• answer the question?	☐
	• give full answers (not just one or two words)?	☐
	• express your opinion?	☐
	• sound interested?	☐

Useful expressions for Speaking Part One

Answering personal questions
I'm a ... / I come from ... / I live in ...
I've lived / worked / studied there
   for ... / since ...
At the moment, I'm studying /
   working on ...
I'm interested in .../ I'd like to work
   in ...

Expressing opinions and preferences
I think that ...
In my opinion ...

I think I'd prefer ...
I'd agree with that because ...

Speculating
I suppose that ...
I would think that ...
I don't know for certain but I'd
   expect ...

Asking the examiner to repeat a question
Sorry, could you repeat the question,
   please?
Sorry, can you say that again?

2.1

Company benefits

Benefits and incentives

1 What is most important to you when choosing a job? Rank the following in order of importance from 1 to 10.

_____ an impressive job title   _____ training and staff development

_____ a good salary   _____ a pension

_____ flexible working hours   _____ opportunities to travel

_____ opportunities for promotion   _____ parental leave

_____ days off and long holidays   _____ a company car

Work in pairs. Compare your lists and give reasons for your answers.

2 🔊 2.1 **Listen to five short recordings. Which of the benefits and incentives in exercise 1 is each person referring to?**

Speaker 1: _____

Speaker 2: _____

Speaker 3: _____

Speaker 4: _____

Speaker 5: _____

3 Read the article about Xerox on page 17. What benefits and incentives does the article mention for employees at Xerox?

This task is similar to Part Three of the BEC Vantage Reading Test. It's helpful to read the whole text before trying to answer any of the questions.

4 Choose the best answer, A, B or C for questions 1–5 about the Xerox article.

1 The journalist of this article thinks that
   A staff at Xerox are not telling the truth about the company.
   B Xerox offers great benefits to staff.
   C people haven't worked at Xerox long enough to know if it's a good company.

2 Where does the company tend to find its new managers?
   A From existing staff.
   B On training courses.
   C Only from graduates.

3 Why doesn't Kim Moloney have her own desk?
   A Because she isn't important enough.
   B Because there isn't space at head office.
   C Because she often travels and is away on business.

4 As well as recognising its staff though promotion, Xerox
   A gives cash bonuses.
   B provides a number of perks.
   C gives unpaid leave to take trips of a lifetime.

5 One common feature of Xerox staff is that they tend
   A to work hard.
   B to get promoted.
   C not to change employer.

Is working for Xerox too good to be true?

What a lovely place Xerox is to work! **Kim Moloney, a client services executive, can't say enough nice things about her employer.** 'It's a very special environment,' she says. 'People describe Xerox as a family and I was amazed at the number of people who have worked here for so long.'

It's tempting to take Moloney's comments with a pinch of salt, especially considering that when you've been working somewhere for only two years, as she has at Xerox, everyone seems old and established. But there's truth behind her enthusiasm.

Take Carole Palmer, the group resources director. She joined Xerox in 1978 as a temp and has been in her present role for seven years. 'Xerox has been good to me over the years,' she says. 'It has supported me through qualifications ... and last year I took part in the vice-president incumbent programme.'

Human resources is taken seriously at Xerox, Palmer says, and the company has a policy of promoting from within (which would explain Moloney's amazement at her colleagues' longevity). The company takes on only fifteen to twenty graduates each year and Moloney was part of an intake who joined having already acquired a couple of years' work experience.

She started as a project manager for Xerox Global Services before moving into sales. Now her responsibility is to 'grow and maintain customer relationships'.

Moloney is based at the head office in Uxbridge. 'It's great in terms of working environment,' she says. 'We've just got a new provider in the canteen and ... we have brainstorming rooms and breakout areas.'

Much of Moloney's role is visiting clients, so she doesn't have a permanent desk at head office. 'I'm a hot-desker, which is good because you get to sit with different people in the hot-desk areas. And you're given a place to store your things.'

Head office staff numbers between 1,200 and 1,500 people, Palmer says. The company has four other main offices in the UK. The nature of the organisation, which encompasses sales and marketing, global services (the biggest division), developing markets, research and development and manufacturing, means that the opportunities at the company vary from service engineers to sales roles and consultants.

Perks include a final-salary pension scheme and various discount schemes. The reward and recognition scheme is a little different, and rather nice: 'Each manager has a budget every year to recognise and reward staff,' Palmer says. 'It can be in the form of a meal for two, or a bottle of wine. It can be up to £1,000. There's the recognition, and then there's putting money behind it.'

Moloney, however, likes the non-cash rewards. 'Xerox takes care of all its staff but it also recognises the people who put in the added effort,' she says. 'It offers once-in-a-lifetime incentive trips, and recently I organised a sailing trip for my team.'

The idea of working abroad with the company appeals to her, and she says that her career goal is to be part of the senior management team. Here's another employee, it would seem, who is in it for the long haul.

VOCABULARY

Expressions with *take*

5 There are six expressions in the article with the word *take*. Find them and match them to these meanings.

1 not completely believe something is true or likely _____

2 looks after _____

3 for example _____

4 participated in _____

5 employs _____

6 regarded as important _____

Asking questions about jobs

1 Work in pairs. Use the prompts to ask questions 1 to 6 about working for Xerox. Look back at the article on the previous page to help.

0 Q: why / like / the company? *Why do you like the company?*
A: It's like a family.

1 Q: long / working / the company? _____
A: Two years.

2 Q: when / join? _____
A: In 1978.

3 Q: was / first job? _____
A: A project manager.

4 Q: what / responsible? _____
A: Growing and maintaining customer relationships.

5 Q: where / based? _____
A: At Uxbridge.

6 Q: would / like / in the future? _____
A: Work abroad and be part of the senior management team.

2 If you or your partner works for a company, ask each other the questions in exercise 1.

The past

3 Read this profile of a company employee. Underline the three verb forms and write each underlined verb next to the correct tense definition.

Steve Bennett started as a project manager in global services and since then has moved into sales. He has only been working at the company for two years.

Past simple: refers to a specific point in the past. _____
Present perfect: refers to a present situation with a link to a point in the past.

_____

Present perfect continuous: refers to a present action that started in the past and is still continuing. _____

4 Complete the information about Xerox and one of its employees by underlining the correct verb form.

The company (**0**) *existed / has existed* since 1906 but in fact Xerox (**1**) *began / has begun* as The Haloid Company. It then (**2**) *trademarked / has trademarked* the word Xerox in 1948 and eventually (**3**) *became / has been becoming* the Xerox Corporation in 1961.

Carole Palmer (**4**) *was / has been* with the company since 1978 and she (**5**) *worked / has been working* as the group resources director for the last seven years. 'Xerox (**6**) *has been / has been being* good to me over the years,' she says. 'It has supported me through qualifications … and last year I (**7**) *took part / 've taken part* in the vice-president incumbent programme.'

5 Read this application for a job. Write the verb in brackets in the past simple, present perfect or present perfect continuous.

Dear Sir or Madam,

I **(0)** saw (see) your advert for the post of Client Services Executive in yesterday's newspaper and I would like to apply for the position.

As you can see from my attached CV, I **(1)** _____ (work) for my current company for over two years. I **(2)** _____ (join) MacKintyre and Co in 2007 and since then, I **(3)** _____ (have) many opportunities to develop my skills. However, I **(4)** _____ (consider) a career change with a new challenge for a number of months and this seems like the perfect moment to make that move.

I see from recent press reports that your company **(5)** _____ (expand) its operations in China and therefore I would like to draw your attention to my degree in Oriental Studies and Mandarin which I **(6)** _____ (complete) in 2006. Combined with my current MBA, which I **(7)** _____ (study) for part-time at the local university, I feel that I would be an asset to your company.

Please also note that my current manager **(8)** _____ (agree) to write a reference and can be contacted on 0207 857 6785.

I look forward to hearing from you.

Yours faithfully

Daniel Lewis

A letter of application

6 Read this advert for a job. You would like to apply for it and have written some notes about your experience. Use the handwritten notes to write a letter of application (120–140 words) similar to the one in exercise 5 above.

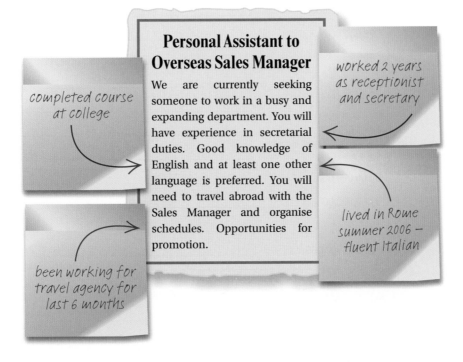

Personal Assistant to Overseas Sales Manager

We are currently seeking someone to work in a busy and expanding department. You will have experience in secretarial duties. Good knowledge of English and at least one other language is preferred. You will need to travel abroad with the Sales Manager and organise schedules. Opportunities for promotion.

completed course at college

worked 2 years as receptionist and secretary

lived in Rome summer 2006 – fluent Italian

been working for travel agency for last 6 months

2.2 Presenting your company

VOCABULARY

Company terms

1 **Work in pairs. Play this game.**

You each have five words. Prepare three definitions of each word but only one definition is correct. For example, if the word is 'turnover', your three definitions might be:

A a company's total profits   B a company's total costs   C a company's total spending

Your partner should guess that answer A is correct. Here are your five words each:
Student A: distribution centre, warehouse, holding company, call centre, plant
Student B: headquarters, subsidiary, branch, corporation, division

If you are unsure of your word, then check the definitions on these pages:
Student A: File 2.1 on page 126   **Student B:** File 2.2 on page 131

LISTENING

Presentations

2 🔊 2.2 **Listen to three extracts from a presentation about Xerox. Which of the words in exercise 1 does the speaker mention when he talks about the Xerox Corporation?**

3 **Can you say all the following figures from the key facts about the Xerox Corporation?**

Fact Sheet   XEROX®

Key facts

16,000,000,000	_____
978,000,000	_____
160	_____
55,000	_____
½	_____
4	_____
6	_____
5,000,000,000	_____
2,000,000,000	_____
1906	_____
112,000,000,000	_____

4 🔊 2.2 **Listen to the presentation again and write what each figure refers to.**

5 The presenter follows this traditional three-part structure for a presentation.

A	B	C	D	E	F
Introducing the presentation	Explaining the structure of the presentation	Presenting the first part	Presenting the second part	Presenting the final part	Ending the presentation

2.2 **Listen and match stages A–F to the expressions below. Write the letter after the expression.**

1 Today I'd like to tell you about …	A
2 So that brings me to the end of my presentation.	——
3 Are there any questions?	——
4 OK, let's move on to look at …	——
5 Good morning and thanks for coming.	——
6 Here you can see …	——
7 Finally I'd like to talk about …	——
8 If you have any questions, I'll be happy to answer them at the end.	——
9 Then I'll give an overview of …	——
10 One thing I'd like to point out is …	——
11 Take a look at this chart, which shows …	——
12 With a turnover of … the company develops / manufactures / markets …	——
13 In my brief presentation we'll begin by looking at …	——
14 First of all there's … / and finally there's …	——
15 Thanks for listening.	——

6 **To help an audience understand your presentation, it's helpful to put short pauses between your phrases. Notice how, in the first part of the presentation, the speaker pauses where there is a / symbol.**

Good morning / and thanks for coming. / Today / I'd like to tell you about / the world's / largest / document / management / company. / With a turnover of nearly sixteen billion dollars the Xerox Corporation develops and markets innovative technologies with products and solutions that customers depend upon to get the best results for their business. In my brief presentation we'll begin by looking at some of the key figures behind the company's success and how the company is structured. Then I'll give an overview of Xerox around the world and finally I'd like to talk about some of the trends affecting our market and its future growth. If you have any questions, I'll be happy to answer them at the end.

2.3 **Listen to this part again and mark in the rest of the pauses with a line (/). Now practise saying the presentation with these pauses.**

7 2.4 **Listen to the presenter say each part of the presentation and repeat it. Notice the intonation and sentence stress.**

Presenter	Good morning	**Presenter**	and thanks for coming.
You	Good morning	**You**	and thanks for coming.

Giving a presentation

1 Create your dream company. Complete the first column of the table with key facts about your company.

	Your company	Your partner's company
Your dream company: • What is your company called? • What product or service does it offer?		
Figures for last year: • What was its turnover? • How was this divided up by region (country)? • What was its final income? • What % was spent on Research & Development (R & D)?		
Structure: • Where is the headquarters? • How many divisions are there? • How many people are employed? (By division? Country?)		
Trends: • What are the future trends and changes for the industry? • What are your company's plans?		

Learning Tip

To help prepare, record yourself giving the presentation and listen to yourself afterwards. Is it clear? Do you use pauses effectively?

2 Now prepare a short three-part presentation for your partner.

Create some simple visual aids if necessary. Use the expressions on page 21 and the information above. When you are ready, take turns to give your presentation. Your partner takes notes while listening and completes the second column above.

3 For your next lesson, prepare a full-length presentation about a company you know well.

Exam Success

When you write a memo in the BEC Vantage exam, ask yourself these questions 1–5 before you start writing. The answers will either be in the question or you will need to invent them.

A memo

4 **A manager has sent this memo. Answer the following.**

1 Who is the memo to?
2 Who will be interested in the information?
3 What has happened?
4 What is happening as a result?
5 What action is needed?

To: All staff   MEMORANDUM
From: James Shepherd
Date: 23 June
Subject: Presentation on changes to pension scheme

Due to the recent changes in government pension laws, the Head of Finance will give a presentation on Tuesday 1 July at 5.30pm in the canteen to outline any effect on the current company-based pension scheme. Staff with this policy are welcome to attend.

---

5 **Study the *Subject* line of the memo above. The writer has taken the four key words from the main message. Underline those words in the body of the memo.**

6 **Read three more memos. Underline any key words and use them to write the subject lines.**

Subject: _____ _____	**Subject:** _____ _____	**Subject:** _____ _____
As you are probably aware, the company is currently considering plans for a new factory in the district of Campi Bisenzio. Models and designs will be on display in the conference room every day next week. All staff are welcome to visit at any time and give feedback.	Following recent feedback on working hours, the Head of Human Resources will give a presentation on Thursday 2 July at 4.30pm in the conference room to outline proposals for a system of flexitime and home-working. Any staff are invited to attend and share their ideas.	Please note that Spanish classes this year will begin on October 16th on Wednesday lunchtimes. Anyone wishing to participate should inform their line manager. Placement testing for new participants will take place in the training centre on Thursday 5th or Friday 6th between 12 and 1pm.

7 **Read the information below and then write a memo to all the staff in your company.**

You are a human resources manager for a large manufacturing firm. To offer staff better health insurance, the company has recently changed its insurance company. A representative from the insurance company is visiting to present the new policy. In your memo you should:

- say what has happened and why.
- announce the representative's visit.
- say when and where his presentation will take place.

Write 40–50 words only. Remember to include a *To, From, Date* and *Subject* line.

2.3 Reading Test: Part Five

EXAM FORMAT

There are five parts to the Reading Test. In this Exam spotlight you will look at Part Five. It is always a short text of about 150–200 words. You have to identify incorrect or extra words in the sentences in the text.

EXAM PRACTICE

1 Here are some words taken from this kind of test. Categorise them in the table below.

has   for   which   because   the   who   are   a   so   do   to   of   and

prepositions	articles	conjunctions	auxiliary verbs	pronouns

2 Work in pairs. Think of more words to add to the table.

3 Now answer the exam questions. Read the whole text first before trying to answer. There are usually three or four correct lines.

PART FIVE

Questions 1–12

- Read the article below about giving presentations.
- In most of the lines **1–12** there is one extra word. It is either grammatically incorrect or does not fit in with the meaning of the text. Some lines, however, are correct.
- If a line is correct, write **CORRECT**.
- If there is an extra word in the line, write **the extra word** in CAPITAL LETTERS.
- The exercise begins with two examples, **(0)** and **(00)**.

A great presentation is like a good espresso

0	Between home and the work, I always stop off to pick up a morning espresso.	THE
00	The only thing that might change about this routine is the coffee itself because it	CORRECT
1	never tastes quite the same. Even if I will go back to the same coffee shop, my 'usual'	_____
2	tastes of a little different from one day to the next. The reason, of course, is that it depends	_____
3	as much on the person who behind the counter as the coffee in the cup. Similarly, the	_____
4	difference in between a good presentation and a great one doesn't just come down to	_____
5	the words and expressions we use or how do state-of-the-art your computer graphics are.	_____
6	Instead, it's the presenter (or the person) who makes the difference, and three things	_____
7	that all great presenters to do: firstly, a good business message goes from the big picture	_____
8	right down to an appropriate level of detail. Secondly, lead your audience and along the	_____
9	way so that its conclusion, when you summarise the key themes, makes them feel like	_____
10	they've just got off an enjoyable ride. Finally, instead take of text on your visual aids, use	_____
11	graphics, flowcharts and visual images. Personalise for them with corporate colours,	_____
12	images and logos. Add that little personal touch – just like the right amount of sugar in your espresso.	_____

Writing Test: Part One

There are two parts to the Writing Test. In Part One you must write an internal communication such as a note, message, memo or email of around 40–50 words.

Exam Success

Before you try to answer, always find out first:
• What is my role in the scenario? (eg manager, trainer, assistant)
• What type of internal communication is it? (eg email, note)
• Who is the communication to?
• What are the three pieces of information that MUST be included in the answer?

PART ONE

You are a seminar organiser. You want to check details for an event next week with your two assistants. Write an **email** to your staff. **Write 40–50 words**.

• Say which rooms you have booked for the event.
• Ask them to confirm the schedule with security.
• Explain that one participant will be late.

Learning Tip

A good way to learn is to swap your written work with a partner. Check each other's work. For this question, say what you like about your partner's answer and use the exam checklist below.

Did he / she ... • include the three pieces of information in the question? ☐
• write 40–50 words? ☐

3.1   Starting a business

VOCABULARY

Types of business

1 Here are three different ways to start your own business. Work in pairs and think of one advantage and one disadvantage for each approach.

> **Sole trader** You are self-employed and set up the business on your own.
>
> **Partnership** You are self-employed and start the business with another person. You are both equally liable.
>
> **Franchise** You buy a licence to trade under the name of the franchisor and you benefit from the franchisor's expertise.

READING

2 The table below lists things to remember if you are setting up a new business as a sole trader. Read the article and complete the right-hand column.

Setting up your own business	Becoming a franchisee
– good if you have plenty of business experience	
– very high-risk	
– many new businesses fail (nine out of ten)	
– suits people who don't like to follow rules	
– for very independent people	
– has the potential to become a franchise	

We wanna hold your hand

Take a big piece of business sense, add some entrepreneurial spirit and voilà! You have a franchise. Starting up a franchise could be a very clever move for those who want to run their own show but don't have the experience or the desire to **set up** in the dangerous and often short-lived world of the sole trader.

But it's vital to know what you're getting into. Franchising is 'the granting of a licence by one person (the franchisor) to another (the franchisee) which entitles the franchisee to trade under the trademark or trade name of the franchisor and to make use of an entire package.

So is the main **concept** behind a franchise that of a compromise between setting up on your own and working for a company? 'Absolutely not,' says Dan Archer, head of marketing at the British Franchise Association. 'That's a ludicrous over-simplification. It is running your own business, but it's taking away some of the risk and bringing

in the support of other people.' He points out that only 0.9% of franchises fail, compared with the majority of individually owned businesses.

But being a franchisee is unlikely to satisfy the most entrepreneurial. It doesn't suit people who don't want to follow the system. William Ewbank, the head of franchise sales at Domino's Pizza, says, 'If you're massively entrepreneurial this isn't for you. It's a discipline, a club with rules. There is some independence – our franchisees can **charge** their own prices although we're strict on menu content. It's running a business with help.'

Astrid Patil, a new Domino's franchisee, abandoned a career as a solicitor to set up a franchise with her husband. The way she reasons it is this: 'Rather than putting all your time and effort into working for someone else, put it into your own business.' Leaving a well-paid, well-respected profession to run a pizza shop at the age of 31 has worked for

Patil. There's a good profit margin and the business has seen growth.

Of course if you do decide to go it alone and start a business from nothing, you could always **branch out** into franchising.

Archer says there is now a **growth** in the number of younger companies that are trying to **launch** new franchises. 'An incredible number of individuals are coming in at a younger age with lower capital, getting a return and investing in bigger ventures.' If the initial **fee** can be raised it's an ideal opportunity to stretch those entrepreneurial wings.

3 Now read about another small business. Complete the text with the underlined words in bold from the article on franchising on page 26.

Tags that can end misery of lost luggage

Globalbagtag was (**0**) set up six years ago by husband-and-wife team Chris and Alison Truelove on their return from a holiday in Australia. The couple decided to (**1**) _____ Globalbagtag.com, which sells secure tags which travellers attach to their luggage. They started to (**2**) _____ £9.95 per tag in the first year, followed by a £2.95 subscription (**3**) _____ for the following years. Customers activate the tag online with their home address on an online database. If luggage is lost, the person who finds it can log on to the Globalbagtag website and report the missing items.

Mr Truelove said: 'We have seen a huge (**4**) _____ in orders as travellers realise they cannot rely on the airlines to look after their bags. It is actually a very simple (**5**) _____.' Globalbagtag is now planning to (**6**) _____ into stickers for items including mobile phones, MP3 players, keys and laptops.

MODULE 3 STARTING A BUSINESS 27

Advice on franchises

4 🔊 **3.1** Listen to a trainer doing a seminar on being an entrepreneur. What advice does the trainer give?

5 🔊 **3.1** Listen again to the talk. Write in the missing expressions.

1 In general _____ _____ _____ you are thinking of ...

2 _____ , _____ _____ make sure that the brand is strong ...

3 _____ _____ , making and selling pizzas might be profitable but ...

4 I _____ _____ you need to like hard work.

5 _____ , _____ the money. You ...

Exam Success

This is the task you will do in Part Two of the Speaking Test in the BEC Vantage exam.

6 Work in pairs. Each of you prepares a short one-minute talk on the topics below. Use the ideas given and add more of your own. When you are ready, give the talk to your partner.

A: WHAT IS IMPORTANT WHEN ...?

Setting up your own business

- A good idea
- Knowing your customers
-
-

B: WHAT IS IMPORTANT WHEN ...?

Your business is a partnership

- Relationship with the other person
- Shared responsibility
-
-

Planning a seminar

I 🎧 **3.2** Listen to a message on a voicemail about a seminar. Complete the information on this message pad.

> Business Circle Conferencing
> Name: Mr Ray (1) _____
> Name of event: (2) _____
> He can't come to the buffet on (3) _____ because his train
> doesn't arrive until after (4) _____ . Please send the schedule
> to his email which is (5) _____ .

2 🎧 **3.3** Vanessa and Kirsten are in charge of organising the seminar at Business Circle Conferencing. Vanessa calls Kirsten to confirm the final arrangements. Add the missing information to Vanessa's notes.

> Notes
> Launching your business online
> 3pm: Security (1) _____ .
> 4.30pm: People with buffet arrive to (2) _____ .
> (3) _____ : I arrive.
> Number of delegates: (4) _____
> Registration and buffet ends at about (5) _____ .

will and the future

3 Read these sentences from the first message. Match the sentences to an explanation of the use of the verb, A–E.

1 We will send it to you immediately.
2 I'm coming to the event next week called 'Launching your business online'.
3 My train doesn't arrive until nine fifteen.
4 I probably won't get to the training centre until Monday morning.
5 I'm going to take a taxi straight to the hotel.

A *Going to* + verb to emphasise a planned decision or intention.
B *Will* for making a (likely / unlikely) prediction.
C Present continuous for describing future planned arrangements.
D Present simple for regular timetabled events.
E *Will* for promising action.

4 🎧 **3.3** Listen to the second conversation again. Write in the missing words in these sentences.

1 The buffet _____ _____ _____ up until four thirty.
2 I don't think anyone _____ _____ _____ before five.
3 I assume that we _____ _____ _____ by nine.
4 I hope they _____ _____ _____ by then!

5 Answer these questions about the sentences in exercise 4.

1 Which sentences are in the future continuous and refer to future events which are fixed and can be confirmed?

2 Which sentences are in the future perfect and say that something will end by a certain time?

6 Underline the appropriate verb form in each sentence.

0 I'm just phoning to confirm that I *will be* / *am* in my office by ten.

1 Don't worry. I promise that I *'ll call* / *'m calling* you back straight away.

2 Inflation probably *won't rise* / *won't have risen* above three percent this year.

3 We *'ll run* / *'re running* seminars every day next week so I can't take any time off, I'm afraid.

4 After that, I *'ll have* / *'m going to have* a rest in my room before this afternoon's session starts.

5 The hotel has a scheduled shuttle bus to the training centre. I think it *is going to leave* / *leaves* every half hour, but let me check for you.

6 Security *open* / *will be opening* the building at eight tomorrow instead of nine.

7 We begin at nine. So by the time he arrives at nine thirty, the first session *will have started* / *will be starting*.

8 He says he *'s going to leave* / *'ll have left* at three to catch a flight even though he knows it doesn't finish until four.

9 I'm sure you *'re receiving* / *'ll be receiving* something in the post in the next couple of days, but I can check with my colleague if you like.

SPEAKING

Discussing a schedule

7 You and your partner are in charge of a training event. Here is the schedule to email out to all participants.

```
New in Business: a Seminar for Young Entrepreneurs

Monday 15th February

9.00—9.30 Registration and coffee

9.30—11.00 Introductions and talk: 'A good idea does
not necessarily make money'

Speaker: Fiona Brewster

11.30—1.00 Workshop and mini-presentations by each
participant

1.00—2.00 Lunch

2.00—3.00 Talk: 'Online businesses — the myth and
the truth'

Speaker: Laszlo Reiner

3.30—5.00 Workshop: Title to be confirmed
```

However, before you confirm these details, read some correspondence and make any changes and notes on the schedule. Finally, meet with your partner to discuss and confirm the final version.

Student A: Turn to File 3.1 on page 126.
Student B: Turn to File 3.2 on page 131.

3.2 Leaving and taking messages

Leaving messages

1 3.4 Listen to five voicemails for Vanessa at Business Circle Conferencing. Decide what the speaker's purpose is in each call.

1 _____

2 _____

3 _____

4 _____

5 _____

A to ask for permission

B to complain about a mistake

C to confirm something is OK

D to request information

E to offer information

F to cancel arrangements

G to request help

H to change a booking

2 3.4 Look at stages 1–7 for leaving messages. Listen to each of the messages again and tick the stages each caller follows.

	Call 1	Call 2	Call 3	Call 4	Call 5
1 Say who the message is for					
2 Say who you are					
3 Give the reason for calling					
4 Spell any difficult words					
5 Request a return call					
6 Leave your contact details					
7 Say when you will be available					

3 Match the following expressions to stages 1–7 in exercise 2. Write the number of the correct stage next to each expression.

0 Hello, this is a message for …	1
A It's …	___
B You can email me at r dot …	___
C The reason I'm calling is that …	___
D It's with regard to …	___
E This is …	___
F So that's M as in Madrid …	___
G You can get me any time between …	___
H Could you call me back?	___
I It's P for Paris …	___
J Call me on 0207 …	___
K I'll be in the office tomorrow.	___
L I'd be very grateful if you'd return my call …	___

SPEAKING

Leaving a voicemail message

4 Prepare to leave a message on a colleague's voicemail. Make notes below.

Your contact details (telephone no / email)	
Who are you calling? What's the message about?	
What action do you want the person to take (eg call you back, meet you somewhere)?	

5 Work in pairs. Take turns to leave your messages. Your partner notes down the key information on this form.

Important
message

message for: _____

_____ **called.**

_____

Message: _____

_____

_____

_____

Action: _____

_____

_____

_____

Taking notes and messages

I Read what people say in 1–9 and write messages. Use words from the spoken message.

0 'Hello. This is Michael James speaking and this is a message for Lelia.'
   Michael James called for Lelia. (4 words)

1 'I'd be grateful if you could return this call on my home number.'
   Call him back _____. (4 words)

2 'I am calling to inform you that the next meeting is on the 23rd.'
   Please note _____. (8 words)

3 'Would you mind checking and letting me know the final dates?'
   Please confirm _____. (3 words)

4 'I just wanted to say that I'm sorry for any confusion.'
   He apologised _____. (3)

5 'The client is asking if it would be possible to put the meeting back.'
   He called about postponing _____. (2)

6 'If you have any further questions, don't hesitate to call me.'
   Feel free _____ him. (2)

7 'I was hoping we could bring the interviews forward. Is that possible for you?'
   Are you able to _____? (4)

8 'Can you let me know if you're available to join us later?'
   Let her know if you can _____. (3)

9 'I'm telephoning with regard to order number 01-X33. I'm not happy about it, I'm afraid.'
   She's complaining about _____. (3)

2 🔊 3.4 Listen to the five calls from exercise 1 on page 30 again. Take notes and write brief and clear messages.

1	2	3

4	5	

Now compare the messages with your partner's.

3 📀 3.5 Vanessa receives a call from Jochen Anderson. Listen and take notes on any important:

- dates _____
- times _____
- numbers _____

Listen again. What phrases does Vanessa use for:

- checking and clarifiying details? _____

_____

- confirming action? _____

_____

- requesting further information? _____

_____

Check your answers in the listening script on page 136.

4 **Work in pairs.**

Student A: Look at File 3.3 on page 127.
Student B: You work for Business Circle Conferencing. Someone calls to speak to your colleague Kirsten but she has taken the day off today. Take a message using the form below.

To: _____

Caller: _____

Message: _____

_____

_____

_____

_____

_____

_____

5 **Now make another similar call.**

Student A: You work for Business Circle Conferencing. Someone calls to speak to your colleague Vanessa but she is in a meeting. Take a message using the form above.
Student B: Look at File 3.4 on page 132.

3.3

Listening Test: Part One

The Listening Test has three parts. In this Exam spotlight you will look at Part One. It always consists of three listening texts which are telephone conversations or messages on answering machines.

In each case you are listening for short answers and filling gaps. There are four gaps per listening. The gapped texts could include forms, notes, invoices or message pads. You always hear each conversation or message twice. You need to listen in particular for information like names, numbers, dates, instructions or deadlines.

1 Study the gaps (1–12) in the forms and notes for the three conversations below. Try to predict what kind of information is missing. Is it ...

- a name?
- a number?
- a job title?
- spelling?
- equipment?
- times, dates?
- business terms?
- other?

Exam Success

- Before listening, study the form or notes you have to complete.
- Use the information in the notes to try and predict what you are listening for.
- Don't write more than one or two words per gap.
- Don't panic if you don't understand everything the first time. You hear it twice!

2 (•) 3.6, 3.7, 3.8 Now listen to the recording and answer the exam questions. After you have listened once, play the recording again.

PART ONE
Questions 1–12
- You will hear three telephone conversations or messages.
- Write **one or two words or a number** in the numbered spaces on the notes or forms below.
- You will hear each recording twice.

Conversation One
(Questions 1–4)
- Look at the form below.
- You will hear a message about a magazine subscription on a telephone answering machine.

Subscriptions form

NAME: Ms Cynthia (**1**) ....

COMPANY: (**2**) .... solutions.

ADDRESS: On record

SUBSCRIPTION NO: (**3**) ....

REQUEST: Send (**4**) .... edition of the magazine.

Conversation Two

(Questions 5–8)

- Look at the notes below.
- You will hear a man calling about changes to a project.

AVH Video
PRODUCTIONS

Notes

Tom Yishan called about the (**5**) .... we're making on the 11th.

They want to delay the filming in the (**6**) .... by ten days.

I've asked to put it back by (**7**) ....

Tom will (**8**) .... that with me when he has spoken to the manager.

Conversation Three

(Questions 9–12)

- Look at the notes below.
- You will hear a woman telephoning another department in her company about a job applicant.

MESSAGE

Message for: Michael

From: Rachel Robins, IT

RE: Job application of Rufus Nichols

Problems:

The applicant hasn't filled in all the sections of the (**9**) ....

She needs the (**10**) .... for his college tutor to get a reference.

Please confirm with Rachel when you have (**11**) .... the interview and she wants to know (**12**) .... the interview will last.

4.1

Advertising

Types of advertising

1 Think of an advert you saw, heard or read recently. Make notes about it below.

- What's the product or company?
- Who is the target consumer?
- How was it advertised? (eg TV, radio, billboard, etc)
- How effective do you think it is? Why / Why not?

Now tell your partner about it. Afterwards discuss these types of advertising. How effective do you think they are?

2 Two candidates in the BEC exam are discussing the advantages and disadvantages of different types of advertising. Complete each sentence from their discussion with a word from the box.

> word of mouth   mailshots   TV commercials   spam
> banners   newspaper adverts   brochures   sample

1   Pizza delivery firms often do _____ in the local area. It's cheap but lots of people probably throw the leaflet away.

2   _____ reach millions of people but they are so expensive.

3   I tend to listen to my friends' recommendations more than anything else so _____ is probably the most effective.

4   People use _____ less and less because they can just go online if they want to find out what's available.

5   It's great when you get a free _____ because you can really see what it's like.

6   I suppose it's good if you're looking for a job locally and _____ are relatively cheap.

7   I'm not sure about _____. When I visit a website, I don't think I even notice them.

8   It used to irritate me but my new anti-virus software seems to block any _____ from my inbox.

3 Work in pairs. Think of one more advantage or disadvantage for each type of advertising in exercise 2. Think about issues such as:

- cost   • location   • number of people who see it   • how long they see it for

Advertising on the web

4 🔘 **4.1** Listen to someone who runs a web-business giving a presentation to a group of marketing managers on how to successfully advertise on the Internet. Which techniques does he mention?

5 🔘 **4.1** Listen again and choose the best ending A, B or C for each sentence 1–5.

1 The speaker compares throwing adverts into the air to
   A Internet advertising.
   B wasting money on advertising.
   C advertising with leaflets.

2 His first piece of advice is to
   A make sure people find you on the search engine.
   B make sure people visit the search engine.
   C set up a search engine.

3 Spend plenty of time on
   A promoting others on your site.
   B creating links to increase traffic.
   C recommending your product on other sites.

4 The speaker
   A thinks email can be effective.
   B is doubtful about using email.
   C never sends marketing emails.

5 It's a good idea to
   A give free samples away at the beginning.
   B make the website free to visit.
   C offer something free to encourage people to return.

A short presentation

6 In the talk on effective Internet advertising, the speaker uses the following expressions to give tips and advice.

The first thing is to …
It's a good idea to …
You can do this by …
Also remember that …
My third tip is (never) to …
Before we finish don't forget …
What might be better is to …

Work in pairs. Each of you has one minute to make notes and prepare a short presentation using some of the expressions above.
Student A: What is important to remember when deciding what type of advertising to use?
Student B: What is important to remember about your target consumer when planning an advertising campaign?

7 Now make your presentation to your partner. Your partner can tick the expressions as you use them.

Advertising standards

1 **Do you know who controls advertising in your country? Read about the ASA.**

> The Advertising Standards Authority (ASA) works to keep advertising legal, decent, honest and truthful. The ASA resolves thousands of complaints each year. It judges advertisements, direct marketing and sales promotions against a set of codes and its rulings are made independently of both government and the advertising industry.

2 **Here are three cases the ASA has successfully dealt with. Read each case study and afterwards discuss the following.**

- Is the type of advertising mentioned common in your country?
- Do you think the advertisers were completely wrong in each case study?
- Have you had any similar experiences with advertising?

Case Study 1: Mrs Q bought a copy of the teenage girl's magazine, Shout, for her twelve-year-old daughter. However, her daughter responded to an advertisement for ringtones offering '2 Tones 75p Each' in large red figures. Further down the page, in the small print, were details of the standard costs for tones, graphics and animations which amounted to £4.50. The daughter only saw '75p Each' in bold and didn't realise the offer was a subscription service. She began receiving lots of ringtones and paying £1.50 each time. Mrs Q was astonished and angry that a magazine aimed at children could contain such an advertisement. The ASA launched a formal investigation …

Case Study 2: Almost 300 people contacted the ASA to complain about a TV commercial for the soft drink Fanta Z. The advert showed people drinking the company's product Fanta Light and then spitting it out. The idea was that some people didn't like Fanta Light but they would like the new drink Fanta Z. The majority of the people who complained said the advert would cause bad behaviour in children. The company said their target audience was sixteen- to 24-year-olds and not younger children. However, the ASA was concerned that young children would see the advert as fun and encourage them to spit. For this reason, it was agreed that the advert could only be shown after nine o'clock in the evening.

Case Study 3: Normally Ms A only buys organic or natural yoghurt but she decided to buy Danone's new range of Shape yoghurts when she saw the advertisement saying that Shape is 'simply a virtually fat-free yoghurt packed with real fruit. And because there are no artificial sweeteners, preservatives or colorants, the delicious natural fruit flavours can really come through'. However, when Ms A got the yoghurts home, she saw eleven additives on the ingredients list. She contacted the ASA via its online complaints form. Eight other people also complained about the claim that the product had nothing added to the fruit …

3 **Look at the comments below about the three case studies from the ASA. Which case does each comment refer to?**

1 The company could argue that all the information was provided.
2 The customers needn't have bought it, if they didn't like the ingredients that were included.
3 She should have read the packaging more carefully.
4 The company must have known that children would copy the images.
5 People should always check the terms and conditions.
6 In this case, the company couldn't show the advert during the day.
7 The rules say advertisers mustn't take advantage of younger readers.

Modals

4 Look back at the seven comments in exercise 3. Underline the modal verb in each sentence and write it in this summary:

Possibility: can, _____
Obligation: must, _____, have to
Advice: _____
Criticism: _____, ought to
Deduction: _____, can't be, can't / couldn't have been
Lack of obligation: didn't have to, _____, didn't need to
No possibility: can't, _____

5 Which sentences refer to the past? How are these modal verbs formed?

6 Underline the correct verb in these sentences.

1 Many viewers think the ASA *should / can* stop advertisers increasing the volume on TV commercials because it really annoys them.
2 A: Sorry, I forgot to bring you the information you asked for.
   B: That's OK. You *didn't need to / needn't have*. I found it on the Internet.
3 They *don't have to / mustn't* use the same trademark as us. If they do, we'll sue.
4 Their lawyers *should / must have* told them not to take it to court because we never heard from them again.
5 He *couldn't get / couldn't have got* through when he tried to call.
6 She *didn't need to complain / needn't have complained* because eight other people also did.
7 Consumers *don't have to / mustn't* buy the product. After all, nobody forces them!
8 They *shouldn't / couldn't* have tried to defend the case. It was obvious they'd lose.

7 Work in pairs. Imagine you are the advertising authority in your country. Write a code for advertisers in your country. For example:

All advertisers should remember that children will see their adverts.
Companies cannot say anything untrue about their product.

8 Consider this case study. What do you think about it? Was the ASA right to stop the promotion?

> Ryan, only 21 months old, and his four-year-old sister discovered a colourful envelope in the morning post and found a sweet inside. Suddenly Ryan's mother heard screams and found Ryan turning blue with the sweet stuck in his throat. It was a promotional gift from mobile phone company Vodafone. The envelope was addressed to an adult but Mrs Richardson contacted the ASA. 'Small children can't read, they are just curious,' she complained. The ASA investigated and Vodafone agreed not to use this type of promotion again in the future.

4.2 Delegating

READING

1 Make a list of ten tasks you have to do this week.

attend a meeting, do English homework, clean the house ...

Think about which of these tasks can be done by someone else. Who could you delegate it to? Tell your partner.

2 Read tips 1–7 below on how to delegate. Write in the missing headings A–G.

A Tailor work to the individual
B Be positive
C Give incentives
D Define the expectations and objectives
E Delegate complete tasks
F Let go
G Avoid misunderstanding

How to delegate

New managers often find it difficult to delegate the tasks they used to do. But getting others to do what you did so well is a key to good management.

1 _____ It should be challenging and make use of their specific skills – skills that you may not have.

2 _____ This is much more satisfying for the person delegated to than bits and pieces. If people feel they have ownership of a whole manageable project, they will usually rise to the challenge.

3 _____ Don't start by saying 'I know you're really busy and don't have time for this, but ...' Explain why the job is important and why you have chosen them. Also explain what the rewards are – possibly financial or psychological.

4 _____ Specify what results are needed, the deadline, and how often the employee should update you.

5 _____ After you have briefed the person, ask them to explain back to you what they're going to do to ensure the instructions are clear.

6 _____ Don't check up on them. Make yourself available to answer questions but allow them space to work on their own.

7 _____ Give lots of praise, helpful feedback and constructive criticism. It boosts confidence and saves time next time.

A bad delegator

3 🔘 4.2 **Listen to a manager talking to a member of his department. Which of tips 1–7 for delegating doesn't he follow?**

4 **Here are some expressions you can use to delegate. Which expressions would help with tips 1–7? Write the number of the tip next to the expression.**

0 Can I borrow your expertise in something?	_1_
A I've asked you because … _____	____
B Let me know how it's going once a week, please.	____
C I'll need a report on this with your findings and your recommendations.	____
D So, let's go through this one more time to check it's clear.	____
E One thing you might want to think about is …	____
F You've done a great job on this!	____
G I've got a job here that will really interest you …	____
H I'd like you to be in charge of all of it.	____
I What are you going to do?	____
J Feel free to call me if you have any questions.	____
K Can you give this priority because they need it as soon as possible?	____
L The deadline for this is next Thursday.	____

5 🔘 4.3 **We can add emphasis to these expressions by stressing one word in particular. Listen to the thirteen expressions in exercise 4 and underline the stressed word.**

Delegating

6 **Work in pairs. Take turns to delegate the following jobs to each other. Remember to follow all the advice in exercise 2 and use some of the expressions.**

- Buy some coffee from the shop across the street.
- Organise all the filing in your offices.
- Attend a trade fair for you this weekend.
- Tell another member of staff not to send personal emails in company time.
- Prepare a report on the effectiveness of the company's website.

Did you convince your partner to do everything?

A report

1 **Read the information and the task below.**

You work in the marketing department of your company and your line manager has delegated to you the task of preparing a short report. You must report on the number of people visiting the company website in the last three months and propose a marketing strategy for the next three months. You have already made some handwritten notes on the information below.

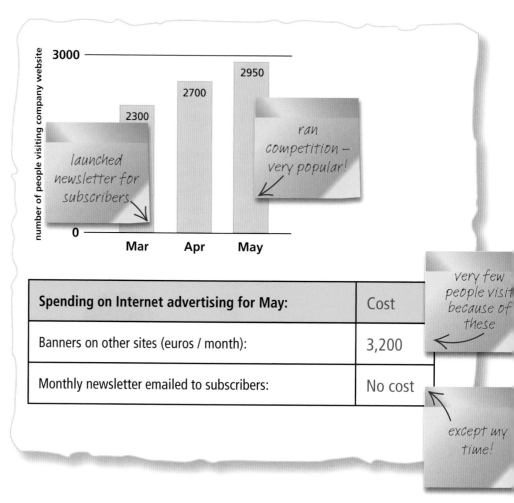

Number of people visiting company website:
- Mar: 2300 — *launched newsletter for subscribers*
- Apr: 2700
- May: 2950 — *ran competition – very popular!*

Spending on Internet advertising for May:	Cost	
Banners on other sites (euros / month):	3,200	*very few people visit because of these*
Monthly newsletter emailed to subscribers:	No cost	*except my time!*

Complete the unfinished report on the next page using the information above. Use the tips on report-writing to help you.

2 Here are more phrases you can use for report writing. Which section of the report could you use them in – the introduction (I), findings (F) or recommendations (R)? Some phrases can be used for findings and recommendations.

It was found that ...	F
In addition to ...	___
Alternatively ...	___
This report sets out to ...	___
In conclusion ...	___
I would propose / suggest that ...	___
The findings clearly show that we should ...	___
As a result of ...	___
The purpose of this report is to ...	___
This means ...	___

REPORT ON _____
_____

Introduction
The aim of this report is to _____
_____
_____
_____ .

Findings
Over the last three months, the number of visitors has _____
_____ . There are two reasons for the increase. First of all, we
launched _____
_____
_____ .

Secondly in May _____
_____
_____ .

With regard to costs, banners have cost _____
but very few _____
_____ .

On the other hand, the newsletter _____
_____
_____ .

Recommendations
In order to increase this number I would recommend that _____
_____
_____
_____ .

3 Choose a website you are familiar with. For example:
- your company or place of study's website
- a website you like to visit

Imagine you have been asked by the website designers to help improve the website. Describe what you (and your colleagues) like about it, say what could be improved and make some recommendations.

Write a short report (120–140 words). Use some of the expressions in exercise 2.

4.3

Reading Test: Part Four

EXAM FORMAT

EXAM PRACTICE

Exam Success

- Read the whole text before you try to fill any of the gaps.
- Often the missing words are part of a collocation or fixed expression.
- It is testing your vocabulary so don't worry if you don't understand the whole text. This may not always be necessary in order to complete the task.

In this part of the Reading Test you choose the best word to fill in fifteen gaps in a text which is between 200 and 300 words.

Read the Exam Success box and answer the exam questions.

PART FOUR

Questions 1–15

- Read the letter below from a local storage company.
- Choose the best word to fill each gap from **A**, **B**, **C** or **D**.
- For each question **1–15**, mark one letter (**A**, **B**, **C** or **D**).
- There is an example at the beginning (**0**).

SUPER SPACE
SELF STORAGE

Dear customer,

WELCOME TO SUPER SPACE SELF STORAGE

Thank you (**0**) C your recent enquiry regarding storage with Super Space Self Storage. Please (**1**) .... below your quotation, which is (**2**) .... for the next four weeks:

Room Size (square metres)	20% Off Monthly Offer Rate From	Monthly
30	£60	£75
40	£80	£100
50	£96	£120

We are currently running a (**3**) .... offering you a 20% discount off your first four weeks' storage. Not (**4**) .... that, we can offer you a further discount of 3% if you pay in (**5**) .... for twelve weeks, or 5% for sixteen weeks.

In (**6**) .... to that, reservations by credit card four weeks in advance are (**7**) .... availability of the room size required. Our terms of storage require a security deposit and minimum of four weeks' rent also (**8**) .... in advance. Both the security deposit and any unused rent (after giving seven days' notice) are (**9**) .... when you move out. Your goods must be insured to their full replacement value. We sell insurance cover; the charge you pay will (**10**) .... upon the cover you require.

Obviously, we would be (**11**) .... if you would like to visit our store to see exactly what we have to offer. You'll find everything you need to make your self storage (**12**) .... as easy as possible.

Please find (**13**) .... our brochure and other leaflets outlining our range of services. If you (**14**) .... any further information or would like to make a £25 reservation please do not (**15**) .... to call us free on 0800 546 7364, or visit www.superspace.com.

Yours sincerely,

David Haynes

PS Don't forget to use the enclosed special £15-off voucher for all packing materials.

1	A find	B enclose	C notice	D reply
2	A representative	B valid	C applicable	D up-to-date
3	A commercial	B product	C price	D promotion
4	A on	B but	C only	D either
5	A arrears	B advance	C part	D dollars
6	A addition	B fact	C special	D well
7	A given	B made	C warranted	D guaranteed
8	A cost	B priced	C payable	D returned
9	A charged	B refundable	C replaced	D reissued
10	A excess	B rely	C hang	D depend
11	A open	B delighted	C here	D realised
12	A experience	B knowledge	C awareness	D opportunity
13	A enclosed	B added	C inside	D requested
14	A ask	B question	C require	D book
15	A think	B contact	C consider	D hesitate

5.1

The workplace

Art at work

1 Do you have paintings and art where you work or study? Do you like it? Does it help you?

2 Read about a company that deals with art in the workplace. Complete the information with answers A, B, C or D.

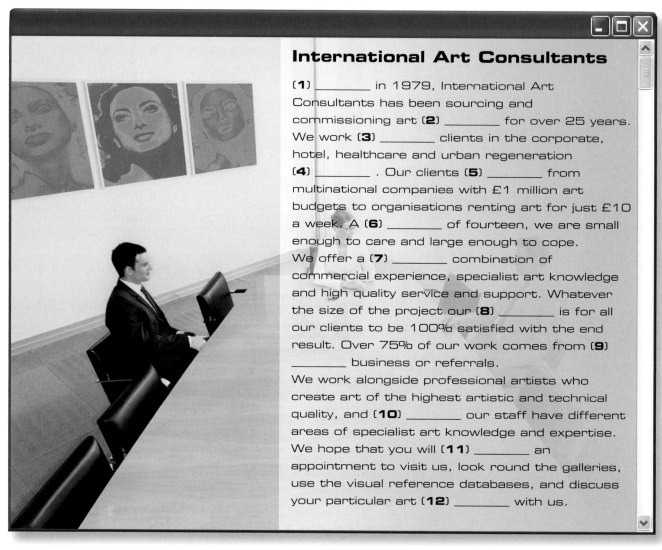

International Art Consultants

(1) _____ in 1979, International Art Consultants has been sourcing and commissioning art **(2)** _____ for over 25 years. We work **(3)** _____ clients in the corporate, hotel, healthcare and urban regeneration **(4)** _____ . Our clients **(5)** _____ from multinational companies with £1 million art budgets to organisations renting art for just £10 a week. A **(6)** _____ of fourteen, we are small enough to care and large enough to cope.

We offer a **(7)** _____ combination of commercial experience, specialist art knowledge and high quality service and support. Whatever the size of the project our **(8)** _____ is for all our clients to be 100% satisfied with the end result. Over 75% of our work comes from **(9)** _____ business or referrals.

We work alongside professional artists who create art of the highest artistic and technical quality, and **(10)** _____ our staff have different areas of specialist art knowledge and expertise. We hope that you will **(11)** _____ an appointment to visit us, look round the galleries, use the visual reference databases, and discuss your particular art **(12)** _____ with us.

1	A Founded	B Set	C Since	D Last
2	A international	B worldwide	C all	D around
3	A as	B in	C under	D with
4	A divisions	B industries	C sectors	D sections
5	A range	B report	C buy	D supply
6	A department	B building	C unit	D team
7	A original	B mix	C brand	D unique
8	A scope	B aim	C outcome	D line
9	A new	B rental	C reply	D repeat
10	A few	B all	C more	D any
11	A make	B do	C have	D attend
12	A insure	B objectives	C requirements	D paintings

An interview with an art consultant

3 There are five main stages for an art consultant in charge of supplying artworks. The following stages are in the wrong order. Work in pairs and number the stages 1 to 5.

- Draw up selection of possible artworks. _____
- Installation. _____
- Select or commission artworks. _____
- Art consultant makes initial visit. _____
- Present possible choices to client. _____

4 🔘 **5.1 Listen to the first part of an interview with an art consultant and check your answers in exercise 3.**

5 🔘 **5.2 Listen to the second part of the interview. Does the consultant normally recommend traditional or modern artworks for companies? Why?**

6 🔘 **5.1, 5.2 Listen again to both parts of the interview. Choose the best answer (A, B or C) for questions 1–6.**

1 If you are interested in having art in your workplace, the best thing to do is to
  A ask an art consultant to visit the premises.
  B look at where you want to put the paintings and decide how many you need for the size of the building.
  C decide what type of art you like.

2 The art is usually chosen
  A by the specialist.
  B by the client.
  C with both sides in agreement.

3 With a specially commissioned work of art, it's best that you let
  A the consultant tell the artist what you want.
  B the artist know what you want.
  C the artist make most of the decisions.

4 The consultant believes that choosing art for the workplace is about
  A everyone agreeing on what they like.
  B having something nice to look at.
  C letting people know what kind of company you are.

5 Why do most companies choose contemporary or modern art?
  A Because people don't like traditional art.
  B Because people don't know if it's good or bad.
  C Because it sends out a certain message about the company.

6 What does the interviewer think is a good idea?
  A To rent the art.
  B To buy the art.
  C To regularly change the art.

Reporting

1 A company is moving offices. A consultant is asking some employees for their comments on what they would like in their new offices. Their comments are then reported. Compare the verbs in the comments with the report and complete the grammar summary that follows.

> We prefer the paintings in our old offices.

> I've always disliked the colour of the walls.

> I'll need a larger desk.

Findings	• The receptionist said she would need a larger desk.
	• 23% said they preferred the paintings in their old offices.
	• The CEO said he'd always disliked the colour of the walls.

Direct speech	Reported speech
(1) _____ (present simple)	**(2)** _____ (past simple)
'We are moving ...' (present continuous)	She said they were moving ... (past continuous)
(3) _____ (present perfect)	**(4)** _____ (past perfect)
'I worked ...' (past simple)	He said he had worked ... (past perfect)
(5) _____ (can/will)	**(6)** _____ (could/would)

2 Rewrite these comments to report them.

1 I am not happy with the arrangements.
   She said (that) _____.
2 We're moving next week.
   He said _____ the following week.
3 We've planned everything.
   They said they _____.
4 I left the company in 2001.
   He said that he _____.
5 I'll call back at tomorrow.
   The caller said she _____ the next day.

3 We can report speech using the word *said*. However, there are other reporting verbs which tell us what a speaker thinks. Match the reporting verbs on the left to the comments on the right.

1 concluded   A 'But we can buy new computers with that.'
2 apologised*   B 'Hi. I'm just phoning to say I'll be a few minutes late.'
3 called*   C 'I'm really sorry that I've missed the deadline.'
4 agreed   D 'Can I take a day off next week?'
5 argued   E 'You're absolutely right that management is spending too much
6 asked*   time on paperwork.'
     F 'So to sum up, the company can offer a two percent pay rise.'

In pairs, practise reporting the comments on the right with the verbs. For example:
He asked if he could take a day off next week.

*Note that we often use *for* + *-ing* after *apologised*; *to say* after *called*; and *if* after *asked*.

Some opinions on art

4 🔘 **5.3** A company is choosing an artwork for its reception area. Listen to five employees commenting on the five artworks below. Decide which artwork each speaker is commenting on. Number the artwork.

5 🔘 **5.3** Listen again. Match the views A–H with speakers 1–5.

Speaker 1 _____ _____ _____

Speaker 2 _____

Speaker 3 _____

Speaker 4 _____ _____

Speaker 5 _____

A ... thought that the picture should be bolder.
B ... commented that it didn't look like anything he knew.
C ... explained what it was.
D ... asked what it was.
E ... apologised for not knowing anything about art.
F ... said it didn't look like art.
G ... argued that the picture should be modern and contemporary.
H ... suggested where to put it.

A meeting about artwork

6 Work in groups of three to complete the following task.

Your company wants to buy artworks for these parts of the building:

1 The reception area   2 The coffee area   3 The conference room

Hold three short meetings. In each meeting discuss and choose one of the artworks at the top of the page for one part of the building. A different member of the group should take notes for each meeting. At the end of the meeting, this person reports back to the group what was said and what was decided. Remember to use reporting verbs.

5.2

Participating in a meeting

1 Read the first two questions in lines 1 and 2 of the article about meetings. What would you answer?

2 Now read the rest of the article. In most of the lines there is one extra incorrect word. Put a line through the incorrect word. Some lines are correct. For example, line 1 is correct and line 2 contains an extra word.

MEETINGS ARE GREAT

1 Do you spend hours in meetings? How often do you wonder when you're ✓
2 supposed to get some real work done? Meetings seem to fill out our schedules
3 and most people would say that employees hate attend office meetings. 'It's
4 one of those anecdotal things that's such hard to question,' says organisational
5 psychologist Steven G. Rogelberg at the University of the North Carolina. 'I think
6 it's a social norm to complain about your meetings.' But when Rogelberg and
7 his colleagues gave in 980 workers one of two questionnaires about their time
8 spent in scheduled meetings and for overall job satisfaction, the get-togethers were
9 not uniformly criticised. In fact, the study suggests that to avoiding the weekly
10 or even daily office gathering may not always be about a good idea. They found that
11 employees who are goal-orientated and whose work does not require much input
12 do tend to be generally dissatisfied with its meetings. But individuals whose work
13 depends on interaction with others and who have somewhat flexible, unstructured
14 jobs are actually more satisfied that the more meetings they attend.

3 Discuss these points in the article with your partner.
- Do you agree with what Rogelberg says in lines 5 and 6?
- Lines 10–14 describe two types of employee. Which one are you?

Verb collocations

4 Complete these sentences about or from meetings with a suitable verb below.

set	give	move	hold	go	take	run	see	attend	reach

1 I'd like to _____ a brief meeting next week. Do you have any time on Monday?
2 As the chairperson, Mike will _____ the meeting.
3 I _____ your point but there's one problem with it.
4 It's another memo from the boss telling me to _____ another of his meetings.
5 Who _____ the agenda for this? It doesn't seem to be complete.
6 Can I ask you to _____ minutes on this meeting?
7 I think we should _____ on to the next item on the agenda.
8 I'm not sure I can completely _____ along with you on that point.
9 The aim is to _____ an agreement on this by four o'clock.
10 We'll begin with Henryk who'll _____ us a short presentation on his progress.

Expressions for meetings

5 The expressions on the left come from very formal meetings. Usually, you will only need to use the less formal and more direct expressions on the right. Match expressions with the same meaning.

0 A   6 _____
1 _____   7 _____
2 _____   8 _____
3 _____   9 _____
4 _____   10 _____
5 _____

More formal meetings	Less formal meetings
0 Can I just come in here?	A Sorry, but ...
1 How do you feel about that idea?	B Let's ...
2 It seems to me that ...	C I disagree.
3 I'd go along with you there.	D I think ...
4 I suggest we move on to the next item on the agenda.	E I agree.
5 I see your point but ...	F Do we all agree?
6 Have we reached an agreement on this?	G Sorry, I don't understand.
7 Sorry, but I don't quite follow you.	H Let's move on.
8 Would you mind telling us a little more about ...?	I I'd like to know more about ...
9 I'd like to suggest that we should ...	J What do you think?
10 I'm sorry but I just can't agree with you there.	K Yes, but ...

1 Study the 'meetings wheel' below. Some of the spaces ask you to say a particular type of expression in a meeting. Work in pairs.

- Which expressions from the previous page can you use?
- Do you know any other expressions?

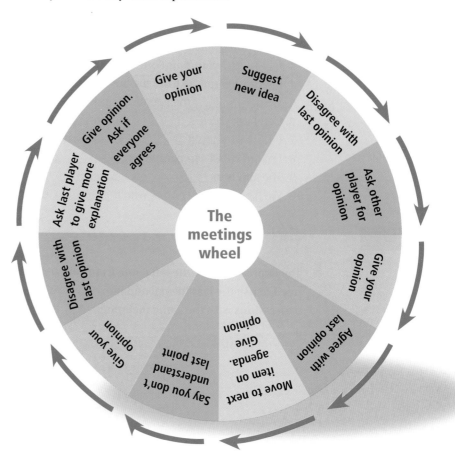

2 Use the meetings wheel to practise using the expressions for meetings and discussions.

- Work in groups of three. You will need a coin and each player needs a counter.
- Each player places their counter on a different pink 'give your opinion' space.
- Take turns to give an opinion on item 1 on the agenda.
- To move round the wheel, take turns to toss a coin. Move two spaces forward for heads and one space for tails.
- Move your counter and follow the instructions on the space.
- Discuss all five items on the agenda.

Agenda for weekly office meeting

1 Should we have more coffee breaks?

2 For the new office decoration, what colour should the walls be?

3 We need a new office assistant. What type of person do we want?

4 We have extra training budget. What type of course do staff want?

5 Do we need more or fewer office meetings?

Report on a meeting

3 📀 5.4 You work for a publishing company. Your next trade fair is in Seattle. Your department held a planning meeting with the agenda below. Read the handwritten notes about what was discussed. Some information is incorrect. Listen to parts of the meeting and correct it.

Agenda

PARTICIPANTS: Robert Samuelson (Chair), Dahlia Zille, Hugo Sata.

DATE: 27th November 2pm

ROOM: 303A

---

1 Conference starts on 8th January. Exhibitors are welcome to arrive on 6th to set up.

HS said it was a bad idea. DZ disagreed and will go on 6th.

2 Travel and accommodation.

DZ offered to find hotel and find flights.

3 Should we sponsor an evening buffet for delegates?

HS suggested a breakfast buffet. DZ disagreed. Preferred lunch event. All agreed. RS to give HS budget.

4 Any other business?

DZ pointed out problem. The brochure has incorrect dates. HS offered to make new price lists. DZ and RS agreed.

Minutes of a meeting

4 Now write the minutes of the meeting using the agenda and the notes you made above. Write between 120 and 140 words, using reporting verbs. Organise your report into these three sections:

- title of report
- details of meeting (who attended, time, location)
- what was discussed and the final action points

5.3

Speaking Test: Part Two

In this Exam spotlight you will look at Part Two of the Speaking Test. Each candidate gives a 'mini-presentation' on a business theme.

1 🔊 **5.5** Listen to the examiner giving instructions at the beginning of Part Two of the test. Are the following statements true (T) or false (F)? Re-write the false statements correctly.

1 Only one candidate prepares a 'mini-presentation'. T / F
2 You can choose one topic from three. T / F
3 Candidates start speaking as soon as they receive the topics. T / F
4 You are not allowed to write anything. T / F
5 When one candidate finishes the other asks a question (so you need to listen carefully). T / F

2 The examiner gives the first candidate the topics on the next page. Once you've chosen your topic, you need to mention the points on the card and add some of your own ideas. Which topic would you choose? Tell your partner why.

3 🔊 **5.6** Now listen to the rest of Part Two. The examiner asks Pierre to speak first. He chooses topic A. Which expressions does he use below?

Giving a mini-presentation	
Starting your presentation	
When ... it's important to ...	☐
The first thing when ... is to ...	☐
There are a number of points to consider when ...	☐
Mentioning and sequencing the points	
First of all, there's ...	☐
For example ...	☐
Secondly / The second point to remember is ...	☐
Something else is ...	☐
The final point is ...	☐
Adding information	
It's also important to say ...	☐
In addition to that ...	☐
You also need to consider ...	☐

4 What is Erica's (the second candidate's) question at the end? Do you think it's a good question? How would you answer it?

5 Now work in pairs and take turns to give a presentation. Each of you chooses from the two other topics below (not topic A). Remember to prepare for it with notes and then present to your partner. At the end, your partner asks you a question.

A WHAT IS IMPORTANT WHEN ...?

Placing a newspaper advert

• The target reader
• Where the advert appears
•

B WHAT IS IMPORTANT WHEN ...?

Arranging in-house training

• Training needs of staff
• The trainer
•

C WHAT IS IMPORTANT WHEN ...?

Selecting applicants for a job

• Personal qualities
• Previous experience
•

6 When you practise Part Two of the Speaking Test, evaluate your own or each other's performance with this checklist.

Did you ...
• spend time preparing and making notes? ☐
• introduce the topic? ☐
• mention the two points? ☐
• add your own points? ☐
• only speak for one minute? ☐
• answer the other candidate's question? ☐

6.1   Recruitment

Employment news

1 Find someone in your class who ...

	Name
• has had a part-time job	_____
• has had more than three jobs	_____
• has only spent one week in a job	_____
• has lost a job	_____
• has had the same job twice	_____
• has taken redundancy	_____

2 Read the three news stories and match each extract A, B or C to a person described below. In 1 and 5 there are two correct answers. Underline the words in the text which give you the answer.

Which person ...

1 has stopped working? _____ _____
2 has started working? _____
3 doesn't need to work? _____
4 has lost a job? _____
5 didn't speak to their employer face-to-face? _____ _____

Text A

Worker receives unwelcome text message

Katy Tanner's cell phone beeped with a startling message – you're fired.

Tanner, 21, had a migraine headache and took a sick day last week from her job at Blue Banana, a body-piercing studio, she said on Monday. She turned on her cell phone the next day to discover she'd been fired from her sales position. 'We've reviewed your sales figures and they're not really up to the level we need,' shop manager Alex Barlett wrote in the message. 'As a result, we will not require your services any more. Thank you for your time with us.'

Text B

Don't call us; we'll call you!

When most people apply for a job they expect to go in for an interview. But not Jenny Jamieson. When a company rang her to arrange an interview they heard her voicemail and she was hired. Jenny came from a singing family and was trained in speech and music. She is now the voice of the company on all its automated messages and call centre systems. 'I suppose I'm always cheerful and smile a lot and I think people hear that on the phone,' says Jenny.

Text C

Car Plant Workers Win Lottery

Harry Lane was one of six employees at a UK car plant who received their £9.5 million winnings from last Saturday night's lottery and announced they wouldn't be going back to work. 61-year-old Harry said, 'I've been retired for two days now. I thought I'd have to work for another four years but this is like a dream!'

Harry's only plans so far are to pay off the rest of his mortgage and take his grandchildren on holiday. No one at his old factory was available to comment on how they would be replacing the six workers.

3 Discuss with your partner.
• Do you think Katy Tanner's employer acted correctly?
• Would you do the same as Harry Lane?

Hiring and firing

4 Put these verbs for talking about hiring and firing in the table.

hire   recruit   give notice   dismiss   walk out   sack   fire   lay off   resign
take voluntary redundancy   employ   ~~take someone on~~   make redundant

give a job	take someone's job away	leave a job
take someone on		

Employment case studies

5 6.1 Listen to five speakers describing what happened to them at work. Match the speakers to actions A–G.

Speaker 1 _____
Speaker 2 _____
Speaker 3 _____
Speaker 4 _____
Speaker 5 _____

A walked out of the job
B was made redundant
C took someone on
D was fired
E gave notice
F was hired part-time
G took voluntary redundancy

Employment issues

6 Work in pairs. Take turns to ask and answer the questions about employment.

1 Do you think it is unethical to lie about your qualifications on your CV?
2 When a member of staff has a problem at work, how important is it for the manager to discuss the problem before making a final decision?
3 How can good communication between managers and staff avoid potential problems at work?
4 If someone gives their notice, what do you think is a reasonable period? One week? Two months? What will it depend upon?
5 What is important to find out before you take a new member of staff on?
6 What are reasonable grounds for firing someone? How much warning should they be given in such situations?
7 Is it ever right to walk out of a job without giving any notice?

Exam Success

At the end of Part Three in the Speaking Test, the examiner might ask you extra questions about a business topic. When you answer, avoid using only one or two words and give reasons to support your views.

Passives

1 Underline the passive form of the verb in these sentences.

0 300 people <u>have been made redundant</u> in a series of cutbacks.

1 He's employed by a number of different companies.

2 He must have been asked to leave after what he did.

3 It is hoped that new investment in the region will generate employment.

4 The news is that they are being made redundant.

5 Michael Jarvis and Kaleigh Macdonald's case is to be looked at by the European court.

6 A number of people were taken on with short-term contracts.

7 This time it's a warning but next time she'll be fired.

2 Now match them to these tenses and verb forms.

Present simple 1

Present continuous _____

Present perfect _____

Past simple _____

Will (future) _____

Present infinitive _____

It + passive _____

Modal _____

3 Complete sentences 1–8 with the passive form using the verb in brackets.

1 If we catch an employee stealing, they _____ (give) a verbal warning.

2 At present, the policy on dismissal _____ (review).

3 I _____ (offer) a redundancy package – I simply can't refuse it!

4 The company _____ (set up) by the family's great-grandfather.

5 The new performance-related bonus means that we _____ (give) a further 10% extra every month.

6 I'm not sure what happened exactly. The incident needs _____ (look) at quite carefully.

7 It _____ (hope) by the whole board that you will accept our generous offer.

8 It isn't like her to be late. She must _____ (delay) at the airport.

4 Complete these sentences about yourself using the passive form. Tell your partner.

• I'm employed by ...

• Currently, the main project being worked on is ...

• I've recently been trained to ...

• The company was set up by ...

• If an employee at my company works hard, they'll be ...

5 Complete this report by underlining the correct form, active or passive.

Report on the dismissal of Ludwiga Chuhova

Introduction

The aim of this report is (**1**) *to assess / to be assessed* whether Ms Chuhova (**2**) *unfairly dismissed / was unfairly dismissed* and if the correct procedure (**3**) *followed / was followed* by her line manager.

Findings

First of all, it (**4**) *has found / has been found* that Ms Chuhova (**5**) *had failed / had been failed* to arrive for work on three occasions.
On the first occasion, when the manager gave a verbal warning, she (**6**) *reports / is reported* to have said that it was none of his business.
On the second occasion, the line manager (**7**) *gave / was given* her a written warning. When she failed to arrive for work a third time, she (**8**) *dismissed / was dismissed* with immediate effect.

Conclusions and recommendations

In conclusion, the manager (**9**) *appears / is appeared* to have followed the correct course of action. However, it (**10**) *recommends / is recommended* that in the future, any disciplinary procedures (**11**) *should carry out / should be carried out* in the presence of one other person. This (**12**) *will help / will be helped* to avoid any similar situations.

6 Do you have disciplinary procedures that must be followed where you work? Are they similar to those outlined in the report?

6.2 Emailing

1 Are you an email addict? Complete this quiz and find out.

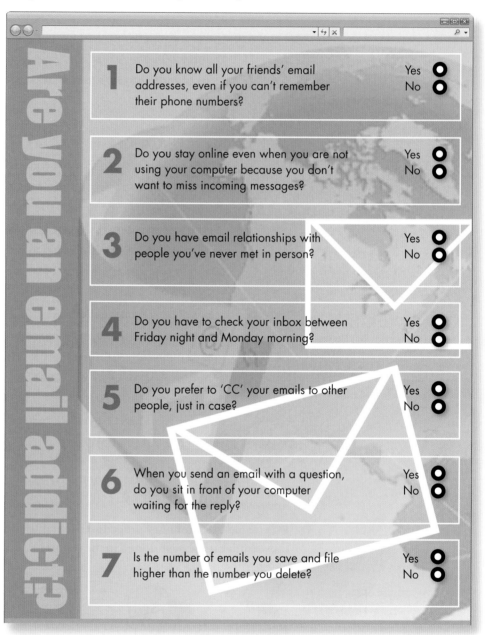

Are you an email addict?

1 Do you know all your friends' email addresses, even if you can't remember their phone numbers?   Yes ◯ No ◯

2 Do you stay online even when you are not using your computer because you don't want to miss incoming messages?   Yes ◯ No ◯

3 Do you have email relationships with people you've never met in person?   Yes ◯ No ◯

4 Do you have to check your inbox between Friday night and Monday morning?   Yes ◯ No ◯

5 Do you prefer to 'CC' your emails to other people, just in case?   Yes ◯ No ◯

6 When you send an email with a question, do you sit in front of your computer waiting for the reply?   Yes ◯ No ◯

7 Is the number of emails you save and file higher than the number you delete?   Yes ◯ No ◯

2 Read the article on page 61 and write in the correct letter, A–F, for the missing sentences.

A This is where we first find out about decisions that have been made, deals struck and the direction being taken.

B In the past few months, 290 employees at a government department have been sacked via their office intranet, while a car equipment firm laid off the workforce by email.

C Then suddenly you send an email to the wrong person.

D They are typical of the average employee who sends 34 emails a day.

E Sending mail CC has only made it worse.

F Two letters were attached, one saying her contract had been cancelled, the other that she should return any work items.

Clicking the habit

Email makes many things so much easier – including making someone redundant. (**1**) _____ In the case of Helen Saxon-Jones, she was checking her inbox from home one day when she read the subject line: 'This email is only to be opened during office hours'. But she clicked on it anyway. (**2**) _____. Unable to believe it, the 29-year-old, who had been working as a project development officer with a charity, took the case to a tribunal. She finally received £12,000 in compensation from her former employer.

But these bosses who dismiss workers by email aren't necessarily evil, cowardly people – they're mostly people just like you and me who have developed the habit of using email too much. (**3**) _____ They meet people and exchange email addresses rather than phone numbers. They email CVs to prospective employers. In a survey of workers last week, almost half admitted they email the person sitting next to them to avoid making verbal contact, and one in five of us uses email just to gossip about work colleagues.

Regardless of the field in which you work, it is a safe bet to guess that your first course of action on any given workday is to log on to your PC and begin checking your inbox. (**4**) _____ We send a question and become offended if the recipient does not respond within hours. We have become slaves to the inbox, dependent on a constant flow of typed communication.

So type-type-type, even when it is unnecessary. Workers type up their every thought and send off emails with tremendous inaccuracy or complete pointlessness. (**5**) _____ We are copied in on emails that do not directly affect us in the vague interests of keeping everyone 'in the loop'.

Email allows us to continue to work at home. Constant access leads to a compulsion to keep the communication going. You're at home, and there's nothing good on TV, so you decide to have a glass of wine and do a little work. As you review your inbox, you start firing off responses. (**6**) _____ You don't want them to read it and the next thing you know you're sending even more emails to try and undo the damage. Another round of emails has begun!

VOCABULARY

Emailing terms

3 **Underline one incorrect word in each group.**

0   check your: <u>button</u>, inbox, email
1   click on: a link, a computer, an icon
2   delete, save, click: an email
3   send, copy, shut down: an email to (someone)
4   log on to a: mouse, computer, website
5   restart, delete, register: the computer
6   back up, save, break : a document
7   fire off, send, dismiss: a reply
8   attach a : sender, file, document
9   type in your: username, icon, address

Now look at the words you underlined. Can you use them in another phrase?

Click on this button to restart.

Internal communication and emails

1 What order were these pieces of internal communication sent in?

1

To: hans.nagle@inverk.com

Dear Hans

I understand there's a problem with stock blocking the entrance. <u>Please</u> arrange to move this before Monday morning. <u>Would you like me to</u> arrange for some extra staff to help move it?

Regards

Inga

2

To: All production staff
From: Valter Rinckes
CC: Inga Palgimi
Subject: Health and Safety Inspection

<u>Would all staff note</u> that our annual health and safety inspection will take place on Monday, 23 February starting at 9.30. <u>I'd be grateful if</u> team leaders would check all exits are clear including the warehouse and storage areas. <u>We appreciate</u> your help in this matter.

3

Hi Valter
<u>Please give me</u> details of the next health and safety check. I know it's coming up soon. If production doesn't clear those exits at the back of the warehouse in time, we'll be in trouble. In fact, <u>why don't you</u> send them a memo?

Inga

4

Thursday 19 February

Dear Valter

<u>With regard to</u> your memo about the inspection, <u>I'm afraid</u> we're unable to make space in the warehouse around the entrances. <u>The reason is</u> that the lorries have been delayed this week so we have stock waiting to leave. I'm hoping that it will be picked up before 9 on Monday.

Hans

2 Look at the underlined phrases in the internal communication and write them next to these functions.

Request information _____

Announce _____

Request action (x 2) _____ _____

Suggest _____

Thank _____

Refer to _____

Explain reason _____

Offer _____

Apologise _____

3 Work in pairs. For each function, think of one more expression to use in internal communication.

An email

4 Work in pairs and write a series of emails between a manager and his assistant. Write the first email and then swap your book with your partner. Write the second email and swap books again. Continue and write five emails in total.

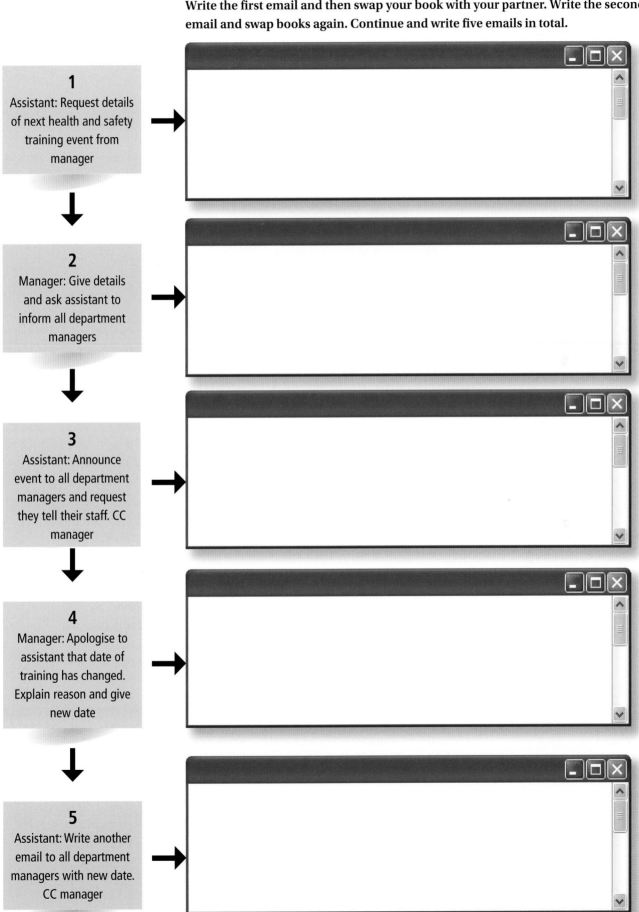

1
Assistant: Request details of next health and safety training event from manager

2
Manager: Give details and ask assistant to inform all department managers

3
Assistant: Announce event to all department managers and request they tell their staff. CC manager

4
Manager: Apologise to assistant that date of training has changed. Explain reason and give new date

5
Assistant: Write another email to all department managers with new date. CC manager

6.3

Reading Test: Part Two

In this part of the Reading Test you must choose the correct sentences to fill gaps in a reading text. The first gap is always given as an example so you have to fill five gaps.

1 On the next page you can see an example of Part Two of the Reading Test. Read the instructions only. Now decide if these statements about the exam are true (T) or false (F).

1 More than one sentence can fit into a gap. T / F

2 You will have one extra sentence left at the end. T / F

2 Read the Exam Success tip box and look at sentences A–G in the exam question on page 65. Underline any pronouns.

3 Three of the target sentences (A, C and G) do not include pronouns. In this case, you need to decide which are the 'key words' and how they can help you to understand the text.

Exam Success

In Part Two of the Reading Test, you will need to pay special attention to words which link the text together. These include words which refer to other words, for example pronouns: *this, these, that, those, he, she, they, his, hers, us, them, which …*

> **A** There are some <u>obvious signs</u> of <u>the second reason</u>.
>
> **C** Larry decided that the best solution was to get help from <u>the organisation</u>.
>
> **G** <u>The next conference</u> is due to take place at the peaceful Dolphin Beach Resort on the Gulf of Mexico.

For example, in sentence A, a candidate needs to ask:

• Where in the text does the writer give 'reasons'?

• What was the first reason?

• What are the 'obvious signs'?

What could you ask about the key words in sentences C and G?

4 Complete Part Two of the Reading Test. Afterwards, compare and discuss the reasons for your answers.

PART TWO

Questions 1–5

- Read the article below about health at work.
- Choose the best sentence to fill each of the gaps.
- For each gap (**1–5**), mark one letter (**A–G**).
- Do not use any letter more than once.
- There is an example at the beginning (**0**).

Too much work is a health hazard

If you constantly try to be the best of the best, stop it. Now. You could be well on the way to giving yourself future health problems. For example, take Larry, a US consultant, who travelled non-stop, worked 60 to 80-hour weeks and still attended meetings at weekends. (**0**) ...E.... 'But I really got a kick out of it.' A period of intensive care in hospital convinced him to quit and adjust his work-life balance. (**1**) .... Headaches, high blood pressure and exhaustion are all the typical warnings that your body gives out. If your boss is irritable and guilty of confused thinking, prepare for a promotion. (**2**) .... A recent survey found that three quarters of UK workers cannot switch off when they leave the office.

Of course, not all our unhappiness at work is due to long hours or ill-health. There are many other good reasons to be unhappy about work. Research by Investors in People has found, for example, that 49% of employees are frustrated by their career progression. (**3**) .... More than a third say that their managers fail to set clear development goals or provide regular career reviews.

So how do you determine whether you are stressed out by your boss's careless attitude or because, like Larry, you are simply working too hard? (**4**) .... Do you take work on holiday and hide the fact from others such as your wife and children? If you answer 'yes', then you have probably crossed the line between everyday hard work and workaholism. This is just one of twenty questions that the organisation Workaholics asks potential members on its website.

The organisation, which was set up by a New York corporate financial planner and teacher in 1983, now has 50 branches across the world. There are no joining fees and the only requirement for membership is the desire to stop working compulsively. Members can attend a conference every two years and share their experiences with each other in a 'beautiful setting'. (**5**) .... If Florida seems a little too far to travel for this, then the 'Workaholics Anonymous Book of Recovery' is available at $15, including stories of recovery by members, a step-by-step study guide and helpful literature to support members in their recovery journey.

A There are some obvious signs of the second reason.

B Larry could have avoided this by looking out for the signs of burn-out or in his case something worse.

C Larry decided that the best solution was to get help from the organisation.

D He or she is probably too stressed and could be redundant very soon.

E 'Occasionally it occurred to me how stressful the job was,' he says.

F 46% of them say lack of management support is a barrier to success.

G The next conference is due to take place at the peaceful Dolphin Beach Resort on the Gulf of Mexico.

7.1

Sales

1 Work in pairs. Compare the jobs in each of the following pairs. What are the similarities and differences? Say which you would prefer to do and why.

- doctor / vet
- manager of a company / manager of a charity
- fighter pilot / airline pilot
- school teacher / university lecturer
- politician / journalist

2 Read the article on page 67. Find out why more people prefer a career in marketing than in sales. Complete the table below with reasons from the text.

Reasons for choosing marketing	Reasons for choosing sales

3 Read the text again and answer these questions.

1 In the first paragraph, the writer says it's easier to start conversations at dinner parties
   A if you are in sales.
   B if you are in marketing.
   C if you are a fighter pilot.
   D if you lie.

2 According to the writer, the truth is that
   A marketing is a better profession.
   B sales is actually more glamorous than marketing.
   C more people are in sales than marketing.
   D there are more graduates in marketing.

3 One reason Ross Snowdon likes sales more than marketing is because
   A it's better paid.
   B you see real results.
   C you meet more people.
   D you can work on your own.

4 It's difficult to attract graduates into sales because
   A many aren't suited to it.
   B they aren't passionate.
   C they don't have the right qualifications.
   D of a false perception.

Not sold on sales?

'Hi. I work in sales.' Not a great conversation opener, is it? Not like being a fighter pilot or a director of Médecins sans Frontières, for example. Unfortunately, a job in sales can't quite shake off its unglamorous image or associations with something rather dishonest. This all means recruitment problems for graduate employees. On the other hand, marketing – a less direct way of selling a product – is rather more popular as a career choice, and sounds better at dinner parties.

Why? Susan Stevens, head of HR at Toshiba, believes that marketing 'retains an air of glamour' and that graduates 'expect to work on creative campaigns with PRs and lots of jollies'. But, on the other hand, sales means 'door-to-door work and cold calling'. Yet this image is misleading. Sales professionals in the UK outnumber people in marketing by about 200,000. This is partly because those who do fall into sales work realise it isn't anything like as awful as the myths suggest.

Stevens says that Toshiba recently had to market its graduate scheme as a sales and marketing programme because 'we knew sales alone wouldn't attract people'. The gamble paid off. Last year the majority of recruits chose sales, including Ross Snowdon, a marketing graduate. 'Unlike marketing, sales is tangible. It has direct impact on a company's results. It's all about meeting people and communicating with different personalities.'

Part of the reason why graduates are often not interested in sales is because it isn't seen as a profession. Clarissa Gent, a chemistry graduate and sales manager at Rackspace Managed Hosting, an IT support firm, says: 'Careers departments don't talk about sales and there is a lack of education about the different levels you can go to with it. I always thought marketing seemed more attractive, but it wasn't the dynamic world I'd imagined. Then I talked to people in sales and realised that it is possible to be passionate about it. It soon became apparent that I was much more suited to sales. Now I speak to customers every day in the buzz of a target-driven environment. It's fantastic.'

Tom Moody, a commercial director for Proctor and Gamble, says that sales can be 'managing millions of pounds of business and making sure the customer's happy. It's incredibly rewarding.' Now there's a convincing sales pitch if I ever heard one!

VOCABULARY

Sales terms

4 Match these words (1–7) from the text to their definitions (A–G).

1 sales pitch	A Making an unexpected phone call or visit to sell something.
2 door-to-door selling	
3 a buzz	B Excitement.
4 a myth	C Business trips with lots of free entertainment.
5 cold calling	D Knocking on doors all day to sell.
6 an air	E Making a speech to convince people to buy something.
7 jollies (informal)	F Something people incorrectly believe to be true.
	G Feeling or attitude.

1 Read about three people's experiences of bad jobs.

The worst job in the world?

A I worked for a firm of architects, which was (unofficially) run by the wife of one of the directors. She was also an expert at creating useless jobs for administration staff to do, such as removing and re-gluing stamps which hadn't been stuck on straight enough. This wasn't as bad as the 'email confirmation form', though. This was her strangest invention, whereby all emails had to be copied into a Word document, printed, and signed at the bottom by someone. When I suggested this might be a waste of time, she shouted at me. I left a month later.

B The most boring job ever is working in a call centre dealing with people for driving lessons. Most of the time it was booking people in with the same three-minute conversation over and over again. Booking a re-test was even worse, because then the people at the other end of the line had just failed their test and wanted to explain why. I lasted three weeks, including a week's training.

C I've had some terrible jobs but in the 1960s, my mother worked in a sugar factory. The packs of sugar used to travel along the conveyor belt and at one point, where the sugar was in the bags but still open, they had to travel around a corner. For some strange reason every sixth bag would often fall over. My mother's job was to stand at the corner, eight hours a day, with a pole to help the sixth bag round. She lasted three weeks and got a job in a café instead. Later she heard they replaced her with a piece of plastic on the corner.

Look at the statements below about the three jobs. Which job does each statement refer to (A, B or C)? There is more than one answer in some questions.

1 These two jobs were the same every day. _____ _____
2 The job description for this job didn't include this! _____
3 This job probably wasn't in a paperless office. _____
4 This job became unnecessary. _____

Describing jobs

2 Work in pairs. Which of these adjectives can you use to describe the jobs in A, B and C?

repetitive   responsible   boring   frustrating   varied   challenging   well-paid

3 Complete the table below with the different forms of each word from exercise 2.

adjective	noun	comparative form	superlative form
repetitive	repeat / repetition	more repetitive	most repetitive
boring			
			most challenging
	variety	more varied	
			best-paid
	frustration		
responsible			

4 Think of three more words for describing jobs and build them like this.

Comparatives and superlatives

5 Study sentences A–D from the texts and answer the following questions.

- How do you form comparative and superlative adjectives? When do you use *more / most*?
- What structure can you use to show two things are equal?

A This wasn't as bad as the 'email confirmation form'.
B This was her strangest invention.
C The most boring job ever is working in a call centre.
D Booking a re-test was even worse.

6 Read what a candidate in the BEC Vantage Speaking Test says is important when choosing a job. Underline the correct form of the word.

'There can't be many things that are as (**1**) *bad / worse* as taking the wrong job, so it's really important you choose the job that's going to be the (**2**) *more / most* rewarding for you. One thing is to think about previous jobs you've had. Think about what the (**3**) *most enjoy / most enjoyable* aspects were. Some jobs are also (**4**) *more / most* repetitive (**5**) *as / than* others. For example, avoid jobs like answering phones or staring at a computer all day. Of course the salary is important and looking for a (**6**) *better / good* -paid job is a good idea but it shouldn't be the only factor in your final decision. Job satisfaction is (**7**) *as / the* important as money, and the more chances for travel and training, the (**8**) *good / better*, in my view.'

Comparing jobs

7 Think about a job you once did. It might have been full-time and paid or it could have been some voluntary work or a job you did for someone in your family. Fill in the first column of the table with notes about your job.

	Your job	A	B
Pay (low- / well-paid?)			
Hours (long / flexible?)			
Environment (the building / equipment?)			
Training (intensive / none?)			
Boss / employer (good / bad to work for?)			
Job satisfaction (high / low?)			

Now work in groups of three. Take turns to describe your job and take notes on the other students' jobs. Then make sentences with comparatives and superlatives about your jobs. Who had the best job? Who had the worst?

7.2

Selling

1 What are the qualities of a successful salesperson? Make a list of your ideas.

2 Read the guide to selling below and choose the best word A, B, C or D to fill gaps 1–15.

How to sell ...

It's not quite true that a great salesperson can sell anything to anyone. For a (1) _____, they might not need it – and sales is all about meeting needs. (2) _____, selling is one of those things that can happen to anyone, no (3) _____ what their job description, so here are the basics.

Step 1 Build trust
You need to (4) _____ trust with the person to whom you are selling. They don't have to be your best friend but essentially people don't buy from people they hate or distrust.

Step 2 Don't misunderstand the customer
Understand the needs of the other person. Then it's up to the salesperson to (5) _____ that the benefits of their goods or services match the requirements. Without that, you have no sale.

Step 3 Ask clever questions
Ask questions to find out what the customer's problems and issues are. Then think (6) _____ what the needs must be. It's often more (7) _____ than asking the obvious, 'What do you need?'

Step 4 Know your stuff
It (8) _____ without saying: know your product and understand the marketplace into (9) _____ you are selling.

Step 5 Don't overload people with (10) _____
You need to know every product specification but your customer doesn't. Essentially, he or she needs to know how it will make their life (11) _____. If later on they want the dimensions, they'll find it on your website.

Step 6 Salespeople are not necessarily born
The classic (12) _____ of a salesperson is someone who is outgoing. But like customers who come in all personality types, sales people can (13) _____. The main thing is to be able to reflect and react to a customer's personality.

Step 7 Be prepared to fail
It doesn't matter how good you are, you will get (14) _____. Sales is full of knockbacks so don't get hung up on it. (15) _____ on to the next customer.

1 A beginning	B start	C customer	D first
2 A However	B Although	C Because	D Whatever
3 A much	B more	C way	D matter
4 A set up	B find	C establish	D know
5 A perform	B compare	C present	D demonstrate
6 A along	B through	C out	D across
7 A clear	B efficient	C effective	D better
8 A goes	B moves	C does	D makes
9 A what	B which	C whom	D where
10 A details	B offers	C discounts	D prices
11 A good	B better	C well	D best
12 A vision	B look	C focus	D image
13 A change	B vary	C listen	D buy
14 A sent back	B recruited	C turned down	D contracts
15 A Phone	B Try	C Move	D Contact

Selling

3 🔊 7.1 Listen to five salespeople and their customers. In each case the salesperson is either following a step from the article on 'How to sell' or failing to follow it. Write the number of the step next to the salesperson and write what you think they are selling.

	Step	Product or service?
Salesperson 1	_____	_____
Salesperson 2	_____	_____
Salesperson 3	_____	_____
Salesperson 4	_____	_____
Salesperson 5	_____	_____

4 🔊 7.1 Listen again and complete the notes about each salesperson's product or services.

Demand falls in
(1) _____ but July is
better. The client might be
interested in advertising
on the (2) _____

The XR5 is a huge improvement on the
(3) _____ model:
 – backseat airbags
 – Travels 0 to 70 in (4) _____
 – air conditioning.

Leather Diaries
 – Available in black and (6) _____ as well as brown.
 – Customer wants to know price for putting company
  (7) _____ on the front.

Points to mention in each call:
 – Warm and Cosy
 – Ask questions about person's (8) _____.
 – Suggest (9) _____ visits to advise on
  home improvements

BEAVIS SUPPLIES
Ray would like to change
the (5) _____ on the
old letterheads.

5 🔊 7.1 Listen for the expressions below. Write the number of the listening (1–5) in which you hear each expression.

A I know it's proved much more popular than ...	_____
B What did you have in mind exactly?	_____
C So is ... something you might be interested in?	_____
D I was wondering if you'd mind answering a few questions about ...	_____
E Perhaps ... could be useful?	_____
F Is there anything I can help you with at the moment?	_____
G Shall I put you down for ...?	_____
H It's a huge improvement on ...	_____

6 Match the expressions A–H in exercise 5 to the categories below. Write one letter on each line.

Establish customer needs: _____ _____ _____	▶	Suggest possible requirements: _____ _____	▶	Compare: _____ _____	▶	Close the sale: _____

A sales conversation

7 Choose an object in the classroom. Work in pairs and take turns to sell your objects to each other. Follow the flow chart in exercise 6.

A fax

I **A salesperson who works for a company renting office space has sent the fax below to a client. Read it and answer questions 1–3.**

1 What are the needs of the client?
2 Is the salesperson able to meet those needs?
3 What are the benefits of the second location?

Dear Mr Rice

Thank you for your order by fax. Further to your request for office space for twelve months,

I'd like to mention that I can also offer you a 10% discount for bookings of an eighteen-month period.

You enquired about availability at the Virginia Walk Centre and offices are still vacant.

However, please note that there is limited parking and some offices are on different floors.

As an interesting alternative, you might wish to consider a new premises called Dockside

(about one mile down the riverside from Virginia Walk). It has the following features:

• a first-floor open-plan office space (75m²) with wonderful views of the old harbour.

• a convenient three-minute walk from the station and ideal for cyclists with a path along the riverside.

• suitable parking facilities for over twenty staff.

Please consider this possibility and note the discount would still apply. A visit to this premises

can be arranged, although I would suggest a prompt decision on this second option.

I look forward to hearing from you in the very near future.

Yours sincerely

Hugo Jones

2 **Underline any useful expressions in the fax.**

A fax

3 Spacesaver, a company which rents warehouse space to businesses, has been sent this fax. Look at the fax and the other information below and answer the following questions.

1 What are Mr Burr's needs and requirements?

2 How can Spacesaver meet those needs? Which requirement can't be met?

3 What benefits of Circular Storage should Spacesaver mention in its reply?

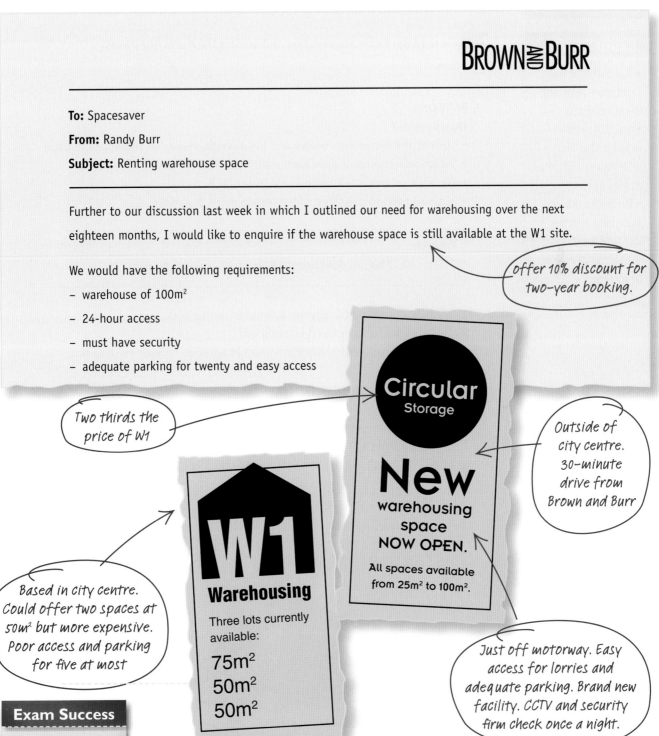

BROWN≋BURR

To: Spacesaver

From: Randy Burr

Subject: Renting warehouse space

Further to our discussion last week in which I outlined our need for warehousing over the next eighteen months, I would like to enquire if the warehouse space is still available at the W1 site.

We would have the following requirements:

– warehouse of 100m²

– 24-hour access

– must have security

– adequate parking for twenty and easy access

offer 10% discount for two-year booking.

Circular Storage

Two thirds the price of W1

New warehousing space NOW OPEN.

All spaces available from 25m² to 100m².

Outside of city centre. 30-minute drive from Brown and Burr

W1 Warehousing

Three lots currently available:

75m²

50m²

50m²

Based in city centre. Could offer two spaces at 50m² but more expensive. Poor access and parking for five at most

Just off motorway. Easy access for lorries and adequate parking. Brand new facility. CCTV and security firm check once a night.

4 Imagine you are the salesperson for Spacesaver. Write a fax to Mr Burr. Propose the alternative location. Use the layout and expressions from the fax in exercise 1 on page 72.

7.3

Reading Test: Part One

In this Exam spotlight you will look at Part One of the Reading Test. There are four short texts on a related theme or a single text divided into four sections. Each text or section is called A, B, C or D. There are seven statements which relate to the texts. You need to match each statement to a text.

1 Look at the four texts on page 75. What is the 'related theme' of these texts?

2 Now read the Exam Success box and answer the exam questions.

Exam Success

• Read all four texts first before matching the statements.

• You will need to read for specific information and detail as well as gist.

• Be careful if a statement includes identical words from the text. It will often be incorrect.

PART ONE

Questions 1–7

• Look at the statements below and the advertisements on the opposite page.

• Which advertisement does each statement **1–7** refer to?

• For each sentence **1–7**, choose one letter (**A, B, C** or **D**).

• You will need to use some of the letters more than once.

Example:

    0   This job does not say how much you will be paid. *B*

---

1 There is a deadline for anyone interested in this post. _____

2 This post has recently been established. _____

3 In this job you can formally learn more in addition to your existing skill.

    _____

4 You will need to manage people under you. _____

5 Your job description requires you to be good at convincing people. _____

6 You must have a degree to apply for this job. _____

7 In this job you must be willing to travel and spend time abroad. _____

A

Conference Organiser £38,000

A newly built conference centre attached to a well-established hotel offers an exciting opportunity for anyone with experience in the organisation and day-to-day running of conference centres. You will be in charge of a team of three full-time staff responsible for booking, scheduling and technical provision to clients. The successful applicant will also be able to promote the centre to local and national businesses. You will need to be self-motivated and have exceptional interpersonal skills.

B

Graduate Media Sales Executives Salary negotiable

A leading guide-to-the-city magazine has exciting opportunities for high achievers of graduate calibre to join our sales and advertising team. The role involves selling advertising to agencies. You will be responsible for managing existing businesses as well as identifying new business. Suitable candidates are bright, numerate, enthusiastic, and have a broad range of interests outside of work. You can create and deliver a professional and persuasive 'sales argument', negotiate effectively and have the determination and motivation to meet stringent deadlines and challenging commercial targets.

C

Marketing Representative £23,000

Large manufacturing company based in UK with factories overseas in China requires a marketing representative. The successful candidate will be based at our main UK office in Reading. The ability to speak and write Chinese is essential. You must be fluent in conversational Mandarin Chinese and English. Other training will be provided with opportunities to take sponsored qualifications in marketing and business. Closing date for applications within 28 days.

D

Finance Manager £28,000

Max Security is a leading provider of UK security services. We also have operations in Kenya and India. The newly-created position of finance manager is to provide assistance in managing and raising finance for the company and help push the company forward to meet its goals. You will report to the managing director and may be required to go overseas to carry out internal audits. You have at least two years' experience of preparing full sets of monthly accounts and payroll. You have IT skills in Logosoft and Sage and are willing to work independently. Experience of working in the security industry would be preferable.

8.1 Training

1 What kind of courses have you done? What do you think makes an effective course?

2 Imagine you are a training manager and you receive information on the two courses below. Read these statements from people at your company and decide which course would suit them.

'I'm responsible for ten people but I find it hard to get the best from them.'

'I really prefer working on my own. I get so much more done.'

'The problem with our company is that departments never seem to know what the other is doing.'

'Why don't my staff do what I ask them?'

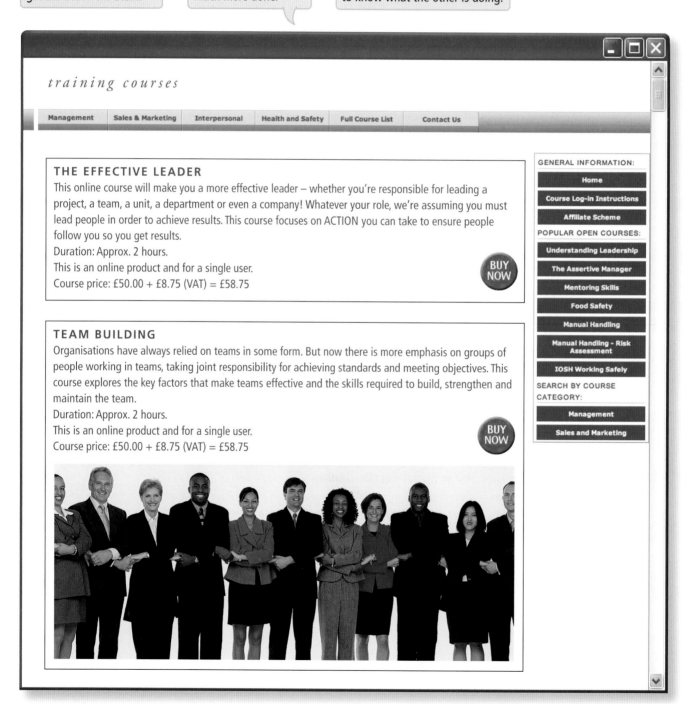

training courses

| Management | Sales & Marketing | Interpersonal | Health and Safety | Full Course List | Contact Us |

THE EFFECTIVE LEADER

This online course will make you a more effective leader – whether you're responsible for leading a project, a team, a unit, a department or even a company! Whatever your role, we're assuming you must lead people in order to achieve results. This course focuses on ACTION you can take to ensure people follow you so you get results.
Duration: Approx. 2 hours.
This is an online product and for a single user.
Course price: £50.00 + £8.75 (VAT) = £58.75

BUY NOW

TEAM BUILDING

Organisations have always relied on teams in some form. But now there is more emphasis on groups of people working in teams, taking joint responsibility for achieving standards and meeting objectives. This course explores the key factors that make teams effective and the skills required to build, strengthen and maintain the team.
Duration: Approx. 2 hours.
This is an online product and for a single user.
Course price: £50.00 + £8.75 (VAT) = £58.75

BUY NOW

GENERAL INFORMATION:
- Home
- Course Log-in Instructions
- Affiliate Scheme

POPULAR OPEN COURSES:
- Understanding Leadership
- The Assertive Manager
- Mentoring Skills
- Food Safety
- Manual Handling
- Manual Handling - Risk Assessment
- IOSH Working Safely

SEARCH BY COURSE CATEGORY:
- Management
- Sales and Marketing

3 Would these courses be helpful for you? Where do the courses take place?

Assessing training needs

4 🎧 8.1 **Listen to a conversation between a training manager and Sergio.**

1 Which course does Sergio want to take? Why?

2 What do Sergio and the training manager disagree on?

5 🎧 8.1 **Listen again. Work in pairs.**

Student A: Listen and list the training manager's arguments for online training on the left of the table.

Student B: Listen and list Sergio's arguments for face-to-face training on the right of the table.

Online training	Face-to-face training

Afterwards, compare your two lists and complete both sides of the table.

- Can you think of any more arguments for and against online training?
- Do you agree with Sergio or his training manager?

Giving reasons for and against

6 🎧 8.1 **Listen again and tick the expressions you hear.**

Discussions	
Giving reasons for	
It's great because ...	☐
One advantage is that ...	☐
Another good reason is ...	☐
You're right, but I also think ...	☐
The other thing (reason) is that ...	☐
Giving reasons against	
The problem is that ...	☐
One big disadvantage with that is ...	☐
One argument against that idea is ...	☐
I don't think ...	☐

7 **Work in pairs. Roleplay these discussions. Take turns to give reasons for and give reasons against.**

- Your manager wants everyone in the department to spend an unpaid weekend in the country on a team-building course.
- Some employees have asked for flexitime and the opportunity to work from home.
- The company wants to replace your English teacher with lessons on a computer.

-ing form and infinitive

1 **Look at what Sergio says in listening 8.1.**

Sorry for being late. Someone needed to speak to me. Anyway, I've looked at those courses you suggested doing …

Match the underlined verbs to the explanations 1–3:

1 Use the *-ing* form after a preposition.
2 Some verbs are followed by the *-ing* form.
3 Some verbs are followed by the infinitive form.

2 **Complete these sentences from the conversation between Sergio and his training manager. Write the verb in brackets as an *-ing* form or infinitive.**

1 I'm interested in _____ (do) both of them.
2 It involves _____ (tell) people what to do …
3 So would you like _____ (enrol) for both of them?
4 Yes, but I can't afford _____ (take) any more time off this month.
5 Online means you train by _____ (use) the Internet.
6 Oh, I see. I remember _____ (do) something similar by post.
7 The problem is that I'd prefer _____ (have) a course with other people in a room.
8 If I do it online, I won't have the opportunity for _____ (network) with people.
9 If I'm working at my desk I always stop _____ (answer) the phone …
10 The other thing is that if you want _____ (do) both courses it's cheaper …

3 **Some verbs can be followed either by an *-ing* form or an infinitive. Look at these pairs of sentences and decide if there is a big difference in meaning.**

1 A: Would you like to play tennis?
   B: Do you like playing tennis?
2 A: Do you like to eat out?
   B: Do you like eating out?
3 A: They've started to advertise for a new receptionist.
   B: They've started advertising for a new receptionist.
4 A: I stopped working there years ago.
   B: I stopped to work on this new project.
5 A: We prefer to stay at home during the week.
   B: We prefer staying at home during the week.

4 **Read this conversation. Underline the correct word.**

Manager Hi, Sergio. Take a seat. (**1**) *Would / Do* you like to have coffee?
Sergio That would be nice. Two sugars, please.
Manager Oh I'm sorry. I didn't remember (**2**) *to ask / asking* for any this week. I only have milk, I'm afraid.
Sergio No problem. I'll have it black, please.
Manager Really? I (**3**) *can't stand / hate* to drink it without milk. Anyway, about your course. We've (**4**) *arranged / recommended* sending you away for a few days rather than doing it online. Is that OK with you?
Sergio Sure. I always (**5**) *prefer / enjoy* to work with a group of people rather than on my own …

Discussing training needs

5 Work in pairs and roleplay this situation.

Student A: You are a training manager. You sent the memo below to all staff. Meet with an employee to discuss which courses will be useful for him or her to attend. Use some of these phrases:

Which courses would you like ...?
Would you prefer ...?
Do you want ...?
Are you interested in ...?
How good are you at ...?
How much of your job involves ...?

Student B: Read this memo from your training manager and discuss which courses might be suitable. Try to use some of these phrases:

I'd like ... / I wouldn't like ...
I'm (not) interested in ...
I'm quite good at ...
I can't afford ...
My job involves ...

To: All staff

From: The training manager

Subject: Available training courses this autumn

Please note that we still have places available on the following one-day courses. All training takes place in our training rooms. Please arrange to meet with me as soon as possible to discuss your needs and requirements in order to enrol you.

The courses are as follows:

- effective selling
- presentation skills
- negotiating by phone
- cross-cultural awareness
- team building
- leading a project
- spreadsheets and databases
- computer skills 1 & 2 (building and maintaining a website)

8.2 Showing you're listening

1 Would your friends and colleagues describe you as a good listener? How do you know when someone is listening to you?

2 Read this article about listening. In some lines there is one extra word. Write it at the end of the line. Write CORRECT if there is no extra word.

The importance of listening

0 Women tend to be very good at it. Men are usually <u>the</u> worse. Not doing   <u>THE</u>

1 it might lead to conflict but using it such effectively can lead both sides to _____

2 compromise and agreement. Listening, and more importantly, that showing _____

3 you're listening is one of the most useful skills as in business. Firstly, you _____

4 can use it to 'coach' and develop your staff by asking them questions _____

5 and for reserving your comments or feedback for later. Secondly, effective _____

6 listening means to avoiding interruption or formulating a response even _____

7 before the other speaker has been finished. This can prevent disagreement. _____

8 Take on angry customers on the phone, for example. A few simple phrases _____

9 to show you see their few point of view will calm them down and make _____

10 them ready to be helped by. So next time you're preparing to speak, pause _____

11 and ask yourself: Have I listened to them? Do they know I've listened? _____

Good and bad listeners

3 🔊 **8.2** Listen to four conversations. In each conversation, is the other person a good or bad listener? How do the good listeners show they are listening?

Conversation 1   GOOD / BAD
Conversation 2   GOOD / BAD
Conversation 3   GOOD / BAD
Conversation 4   GOOD / BAD

4 Read these expressions. Which expressions would you use to show you're listening?

Let me check I've understood you.	☐
So what you're saying is ... Is that right?	☐
Well, of course the answer is simple, isn't it?	☐
Let me just stop you there.	☐
I see what you mean.	☐
That's interesting.	☐
I see.	☐
Can I tell you what I think?	☐
Why do you think that is?	☐
Really?	☐
Well, what you need to do is ...	☐

5 🔊 **8.2** Listen again. Write the number of the conversation after each expression in exercise 4. Which expression don't you hear?

Showing you're listening

6 Work in pairs and practise using the expressions to show you're listening. Take turns to talk about the following topics for one minute. The other person uses the phrases to show they are listening.

- Describe what you did after work last night.
- Explain a difficulty or problem you are currently having with your work.
- Complain about something you have recently bought.

7 In Part Three of the BEC Vantage Speaking Test you have a conversation with the other candidate and the examiner. When the other candidate is speaking it's important to show you are listening.

Look at this task from the exam. Practise discussing the topic for four minutes. Use the expressions in exercise 4.

> **Training courses**
>
> Your company has decided to offer IT training for its employees.
>
> Your boss wants you to organise it.
>
> Discuss the situation together, and decide:
> - how staff will be selected for the training course
> - how to measure their achievement

Linking phrases

1 **You work for a training company and receive this letter. In which paragraph do you find out …**

- the purpose of the letter?
- what happened?
- what action the sender requires?

1st May

Dear Mr Le Fevre

Following the recent experiences of two of my staff with your training company, I have decided to send you some feedback based on their comments.

On the 25th April, they attended a two-day computer course in creating PowerPoint presentations. **However**, on the first day the trainer arrived 30 minutes late, which was followed by a further delay **due to** a room change. **As a result of** this nearly 90 minutes was missed. **In addition to** this, my staff inform me that the approach of the trainer was to let participants 'discover' solutions to problems rather than being told what to do.

Despite having been very satisfied with your services in the past I may have to reconsider sending staff in the future. I would be grateful to hear any comments you have to make either by phone or in writing.

I look forward to hearing from you.

Yours sincerely

A Heneage

Mrs A Heneage
Human Resources

Learning Tip

Underline any useful expressions in the letter which you would like to use in your own writing.

2 **Look at the words in bold in the letter. Write them into this table.**

Cause and effect	Contrasting	Additional information
because of	(4) _____	(6) _____
(1) _____	Nevertheless	Furthermore
(2) _____	(5) _____	Moreover
(3) _____	(verb + … -*ing*)	

3 **Complete sentences 1–6 with a suitable word or phrase from the table.**

1 I am writing _____ a problem with a product I recently bought from you.

2 The advert contains misleading information. _____, it is unsuitable for children.

3 I have complained about this twice before. _____, you have continually taken no action to resolve the issue.

4 _____ having written to them, she has received no reply.

5 We will no longer use your services in the future. _____ we will be contacting our lawyers to discuss possible legal action.

6 _____ further increases in your prices, we are changing supplier.

Responding to a letter of complaint

4 8.3 As a result of Mrs Heneage's letter, Mr Le Fevre calls Fred Perrot, who is in charge of computer training. Listen to the call and make notes about the reasons for the problems outlined in Mrs Heneage's letter.

5 Now complete Mr Le Fevre's reply to Mrs Heneage using the information in your notes from exercise 4.

Dear Mrs Heneage

With regard to your concerns about the PowerPoint course on (1) _____ _____, I have now spoken to my head of computer training and as a result I am in a position to respond.

Unfortunately, and due to circumstances beyond our control on that day, the head of training (2) _____. As a result (3) _____ and he was somewhat late. For this I apologise, but because of this delay (4) _____ _____ .

Secondly, there was a room change which was due to the fact that (5) _____ _____.

Finally, our approach to training has always been based on a (6) '_____ _____ approach'.

Moreover, it has always received (7) _____.

Following this letter, I would like to suggest a meeting at your convenience to discuss any remaining issues and your future training needs ...

A letter of complaint

6 Work in pairs. You will write a letter to each other and then write the reply.

You recently stayed at a hotel. Your partner is the manager. Read the notes on the problems.

- There was no record of the booking at reception – I waited 45 minutes.
- The meeting room was double-booked – had to meet clients in smaller room.
- The towels were not changed in the bathroom overnight – room service said this was hotel policy based on 'environmental reasons'.

Write a letter to the hotel manager (your partner). Write 120–140 words using appropriate linking words or expressions.

Swap letters with your partner. Now you are the hotel manager. Write a reply to the letter. Respond to each complaint, again using appropriate linking words or phrases.

8.3

Listening Test: Part Two

In this Exam spotlight you will look at Part Two of the Listening Test.

1 Look at the instructions from the exam on the opposite page, then read these statements about what you are expected to do. One of the statements is false (F). Which one?

1 There are two parts to the question. T / F
2 Each part consists of six recordings. T / F
3 You have eight items to choose from. T / F
4 The eight items are all on the same theme, eg job titles, places, purposes, etc. T / F
5 You will not use three of the items. T / F

2 In this part of the exam, you will always need to take into account the following.

1 What is the purpose of the speaker? What is his / her aim?
2 What is the role (job, position) of the speaker?
3 What opinion is he / she expressing?
4 What key vocabulary does he / she use?

This is what the two speakers say in the recordings for questions 1 and 6. Try to answer the four questions above for each speaker.

1

> Actually, it didn't tell me more than I already do. I suppose the parts on how to answer questions and working on convincing people was OK. But how to stand and when to use your hands seemed a bit excessive. And when he talked about visual aids I wondered if everyone else thought it was as pointless as me.

6

> Hi Joe. I'm just phoning to say I'll be in at three o'clock as planned. They had said there would be problems on the planes because of a strike but it seems to be OK now so I'll see you tomorrow.

3 🎧 8.4, 8.5 **Now answer the exam questions.**

Exam Success

• Read through the whole question.
• Think about the kinds of words or phrases you might hear for each item.
• Remember that you hear each listening twice.

PART TWO
Questions 1–10

Section One
(Questions 1–5)

- You will hear five short recordings.
- For each recording, decide which training course the speaker is referring to.
- Write one letter (**A–H**) next to the number of the recording.
- Do not use any letter more than once.
- You will hear the recordings twice.

1		**A**	Managing teams
		B	Using PowerPoint
2		**C**	Sales on the telephone
		D	Effective presentations
3		**E**	Doing business with other cultures
		F	Report writing
4		**G**	Marketing on the web
		H	Interviewing and staff selection
5			

Section Two
(Questions 6–10)

- You will hear another five short recordings.
- Each speaker is on the phone.
- For each recording, decide what the main reason for the call is.
- Write one letter (**A–H**) next to the number of the recording.
- Do not use any letter more than once.
- You will hear the recordings twice.

6		**A**	to complain
		B	to explain a delay
7		**C**	to ask for information
		D	to confirm arrangements
8		**E**	to report on plans
		F	to ask for confirmation
9		**G**	to request help
		H	to speak to someone else
10			

9.1   Branding

READING

1 What is your favourite brand of ...

- coffee?
- soap?
- clothes?

Tell your partner and explain why you choose that particular brand. Is your choice affected by the colour, packaging, advertising, price, logo? Do you ever buy a product or service because of its smell?

2 Read the article on page 87 and write in the correct letter, A–G, for the missing phrases.

A where the odour of waffle-cones were released into the air to encourage visitors to an out-of-the-way ice cream shop

B that his grandmother used to make

C which typically includes more than six smells

D whose recently-introduced cell phone keypad was lavender-scented

E when it began twelve years ago

F why so many companies are now associating brands with a scent

G who walk around reception will get a whiff of a chocolate chip cookie

SPEAKING

Discussing branding

3 Try to complete the sentences below about what you have read. Tell your partner what you think.

- One thing that interests me about this is ...
- One thing that surprises me is ...
- One thing that I find hard to believe is ...

4 What smell could you use to brand the following? You can use the suggestions in the pictures.

- your company's product or service
- your school or college
- a new range of clothing
- bicycles
- a language course

What's that smell?

David Van Epps opens his briefcase and touches several of the 72 bottles inside. 'Here's one you'll like,' he says, taking the top off one. He dips a paper strip inside and waves it under his nose, breathing in deeply. It smells of sugar and butter like the 'sugar cookies' (1) _____. It also makes him think of money: sugar cookies is only one of 1,480 fragrances sold by Van Epps' company ScentAir Technologies and used to improve brand identity.

Fragrance is as much a marketing tool these days as a logo, a slogan or a jingle. Sony puts its customers 'in the mood' for buying in its stores with the smell of vanilla and mandarin. At some Doubletree Hotels guests (2) _____. And Proctor and Gamble has experimented with ScentAir scents to attract shoppers to displays in stores, says Van Epps. 'What's better than having a brand people want to use because of fragrance?'

ScentAir first started putting that attitude into bottles (3) _____. ScentAir will charge as much as $25,000 to create a custom blend, (4) _____. This year turnover has quadrupled as more marketers use scents to distinguish their brands.

Once a client selects a scent, ScentAir puts the liquid aroma in a cartridge that fits inside a device with a fan which pushes the smell into the air. You control the strength with a dial. Monthly refills are $100 per device.

Some companies want to make shoppers wait around longer in the hope they will spot something to buy. It seems to have worked at the Hard Rock Hotel in Orlando, (5) _____. Sales jumped 45% in the first six months after a ScentAir device was installed. Westin Hotels and Resorts contacted ScentAir for a white tea fragrance to put in its 127 properties. Added to this, the hotels have just started selling white tea-scented items, including $36 candles.

Alan Hirsch of the Smell and Taste Treatment and Research Foundation in Chicago explains the reason (6) _____. 'Smell has a greater impact on purchasing than everything else combined. If something smells good, the product is perceived as good.' There's LG Electronics (7), _____, or the cherry smell from billboards advertising a new shampoo from L'Oreal. All we need now is a PC that can pick up aromas from websites.

Relative clauses

We often add information or more detail to the main clause of the sentence. For example, the speaker may want to say what type of company he works for:

ScentAir is a company which sells scents.

```
|-------------------------|-------------------------|
        Main clause              Relative clause
```

1 Complete the defining relative clauses in these sentences with a word from the box.

> when   where   why   which   who   whose

1 The new product _____ goes on sale next month isn't ready yet.
2 The turnover was just under half a million _____ it was first founded in 1985. Now it's a hundred million.
3 The people _____ work for us are all highly qualified.
4 We like to think we're a supportive company _____ staff are loyal.
5 Let me explain some of the reasons _____ we're making these changes.
6 The company _____ I used to work is closing down, apparently.

2 Underline the two relative clauses in this extract from a report.

We're a Swedish company which has controlling shares in three subsidiaries and a large stake in one smaller division. It is recommended therefore that we focus our financial interests on the smaller subsidiary, which incidentally is also based in Sweden.

3 Work in pairs and answer these questions about relative clauses.

1 Which relative clause – defining or non-defining – adds necessary information?
2 Which relative clause – defining or non-defining – adds extra but non-essential information?
3 What punctuation do you need with a non-defining relative clause?
4 Look back at the relative clauses in the article *What's that smell?* Which are defining and which are non-defining?
5 In defining relative clauses you can replace *which* or *who* with another pronoun. What is the pronoun?

4 Add the second sentence to the first using the word in brackets.

0 (which) I work for a large multinational based in Sydney. We employ over three thousand people.
  I work for a large multinational based in Sydney which employs over three thousand people.

1 (who) Let me introduce you to David. He's the director of our company.
  _____

2 (where) This is the main factory. We produce car parts.
  _____

3 (which) This is our latest product. It's also our biggest seller.
  _____

4 (when) The company had a turnover of about a million euros in 2004. It was founded in 2004. _____

5 Complete the relative clauses to make sentences about you.

- I work for a company which ...
- I study at a college / school that ...
- The best kind of boss is someone who ...
- I first applied for this job / course when ...
- In the future I'd like to work in a country where ...
- ... is the reason why I'm studying English.

6 Combine the two sentences, using a non-defining relative clause.

0 David Van Epps sells over 1,480 fragrances. His favourite smell is chocolate chip cookie.
David Van Epps, whose favourite smell is chocolate chip cookie, sells over 1,480 fragrances.

1 My company has offices all over the world. It's based in Sydney.

_____

2 Mrs Sayers says she has an appointment with you. She's waiting in reception.

_____

_____

3 The man called this morning to see if we had his briefcase. We found his briefcase last night.

_____

_____

4 The report is in your in-tray. I've just finished it.

_____

READING

7 Read about luxury brands in China. Each line contains one mistake (including punctuation). Correct it.

Chinese luxury obsession

0 When ~~that~~ many people visit cities in China, they are still surprised to see the luxury

00 brands ~~who~~ *which* normally fill the fashion boutiques of New York and Paris. But in a

1 country which more and more young people have become big-spending consumers,

2 the world's top brands attract twenty- and thirty-somethings what, in a recent survey,

3 say they want to 'seize every opportunity to enjoy life.' Take Miss Yu, who's monthly

4 salary is 5,000 yuan working as a journalist. She regularly stops by the boutiques where,

5 you can find Louis Vuitton or Gucci. She explains the reason when: 'I think a bag worth 10,000 yuan

6 is more suitable for me than 100 bags at 100 yuan each.' And her fashion collection, whose includes

7 names such as Chanel, Burberry and Prada, is far from unique in a country why the proportion

8 of luxury goods purchased nowadays, is 40% compared to only 4% globally.

9.2 Getting through

Automated voicemail systems

1 Do you agree with the views in this article? What does your partner think?
Study the graph. At what stage (10–0) would you normally hang up?

Text messages interrupt our lunch breaks and pointless emails fill our
inboxes, but a recent survey says that the majority of people rate
automated voicemail systems and the lack of a human voice on the phone
as modern communication's worst invention.

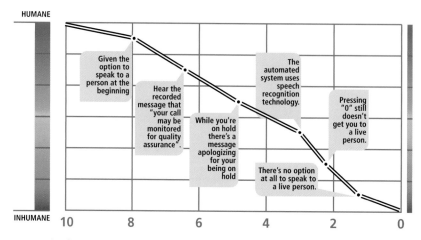

HUMANE

Given the option to speak to a person at the beginning

Hear the recorded message that "your call may be monitored for quality assurance".

While you're on hold there's a message apologizing for your being on hold

The automated system uses speech recognition technology.

There's no option at all to speak to a live person.

Pressing "0" still doesn't get you to a live person.

INHUMANE   10   8   6   4   2   0

On a scale of 1–10, how inhumane can an automated voicemail system be?

2 🎧 9.1 Listen to someone dealing with an automated voice system.

  1 What is the name of the company?
  2 What number does the caller press?
  3 Which stage of the graph does the caller reach before he puts the phone down?

3 🎧 9.2 Another person speaks to an operator at GH Loans Customer Care.
Complete the form below with the caller's information.

Caller's name: (1) _____   **GH Customer Care**
Account No: (2) _____
Date of birth: (3) _____

Enquiry:
The caller paid part of her
(4) _____ but it hasn't appeared
on the (5) _____ . It was for the
amount of (6) _____ .

Action:
Call her back on (7) _____ at
(8) _____ .

Telephone words

4 9.1, 9.2 **Replace the words in bold in sentences 1–10 with a word or words from the box. Then listen again to the conversations from exercises 2 and 3 and check.**

suit call / back bear with me So that was put / through
hold unavailable take take one put / on hold

1 All of our operators are currently **too busy** to **answer** your call.

_____ _____

2 Please **wait**. _____
3 Could you **connect me** to someone …? _____ me _____
4 **Wait a** moment, please. _____
5 Can I **write down** your name, please? _____
6 Can you **wait for me** for a second? _____
7 I'm just going to **make** you **wait**. _____
8 Can I **get back to you**? _____ you _____
9 **Let me read that back to you. It's** zero one seven, two double four, three nine two nine. _____
10 When would **be convenient for** you? _____

5 We often use phrasal verbs on the telephone. Notice how the position of the object can change with different types of phrasal verbs:

(1) The object separates the verb from the particle: Can you put me through? (✓) Can you put through me? (✗) (2) The object follows the phrasal verb: Can you bear me with? (✗) Can you bear with me? (✓)	(3) The object can separate or follow the phrasal verb: Can you pass on this message to him? (✓) Can you pass this message on to him? (✓) (4) And note that some (intransitive) phrasal verbs don't take an object. Speak up! I can't hear you. (✓) Speak up you! (✗)

Write the missing particle from the box in the correct position to complete each sentence. There might be two possible answers.

back on back up on out up forward back ~~down~~

0 Please don't put the phone.   *down*
1 Let me call you later.
2 Let me read that to you.
3 I'm just looking his number on the computer.
4 Do you mind if we put the meeting to Tuesday?
5 We'll bring the schedule by a week.
6 Hold a moment.
7 Sorry, the battery on my mobile is about to run.
8 Sorry, he's tied with something at the moment. Can I help?
9 I'm just putting you hold for a moment.

Making phone calls

6 Work in pairs and practise making some telephone calls. Try to use some of the expressions and phrasal verbs on this page.

Student A: Look at File 9.1 on page 127.   Student B: Look at File 9.2 on page 132.

Email marketing

1 Do you often receive these kinds of email in your inbox? Do you open or delete them?

Become an online marketer – TEACH YOURSELF IN JUST 2 HOURS!
IMPORTANT ! Earn Profits ... Without Doing Anything – no training required

2 Read this article about an email marketer and answer questions 1–3.

Every month 7,000 people receive email newsletters from Dr Mani Sivasubramanian. In glorious italics, capitals, underlining and bold, the subject lines shout: '**Explode Your Online Marketing Profits** – in Just **14** Days!' or 'IMPORTANT Earn Profits ... <u>Without Doing Anything Different!</u>'

But before you delete this spam from your inbox, Dr Mani, as he prefers to be called, gives online help and advice about marketing as well as working as a paediatric heart surgeon in Chennai, India. He donates up to 50% of his profits from selling marketing expertise to the Children's Heart Foundation, which he created to provide heart surgery to poor Indian children.

Sivasubramanian first discovered the Internet as a surgical student in 1996. Two years later, he started selling medical information online. Later he realized he could pass on his online marketing expertise as well – which he does now in fourteen different email marketing newsletters, with tips on how to become an online marketer. Last year he took home $250,000 from his online work, while still working up to 50 hours a week at the Institute of Child Health and Hospital for Sick Children. His foundation took about $10,000, which has helped to pay for thirteen surgeries across India.

1 Why does Dr Mani send email newsletters?
   A To give medical advice.
   B To give marketing advice.
   C To advertise his charity.

2 In 1998, Dr Mani ...
   A started sending marketing newsletters.
   B started selling medical information.
   C set up the Children's Heart Foundation.

3 The quarter of a million dollars from his marketing work ...
   A were his earnings.
   B went to his foundation.
   C paid for new surgeries.

3 Now you have read about Dr Mani, would you open or delete an email from him?

4 Work in pairs or groups of three. Your company or place of study is planning to publish a four-page newsletter once every three months as part of its marketing strategy. You have been asked to help with the planning.

Discuss the situation together and decide
- what kind of articles and features the newsletter will contain
- who the readers of your newsletter will be and how it will be delivered; for example, will it be sent by email?

Correcting and rewriting

5 Read these guidelines on using email at work. Complete the text with words from the first five lines of the article about Dr Mani on page 92.

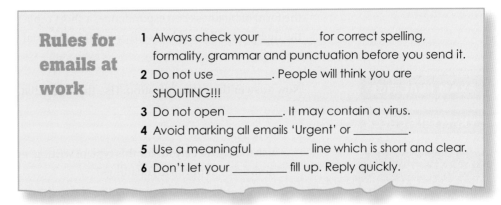

Rules for emails at work

1 Always check your _____ for correct spelling, formality, grammar and punctuation before you send it.
2 Do not use _____. People will think you are SHOUTING!!!
3 Do not open _____. It may contain a virus.
4 Avoid marking all emails 'Urgent' or _____.
5 Use a meaningful _____ line which is short and clear.
6 Don't let your _____ fill up. Reply quickly.

6 Work in pairs. Think of two more useful rules for emails. Compare them with the rest of the class.

7 Which of the rules in exercise 5 were broken by the person who wrote this email?

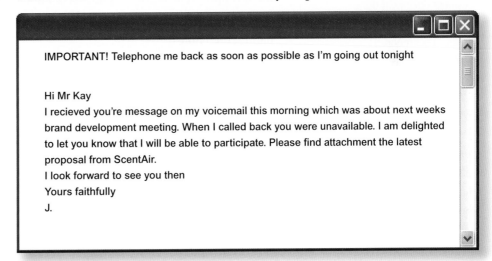

IMPORTANT! Telephone me back as soon as possible as I'm going out tonight

Hi Mr Kay
I recieved you're message on my voicemail this morning which was about next weeks brand development meeting. When I called back you were unavailable. I am delighted to let you know that I will be able to participate. Please find attachment the latest proposal from ScentAir.
I look forward to see you then
Yours faithfully
J.

8 Work in pairs and re-draft the email.

9.3

Writing Test: Part Two

EXAM FORMAT

EXAM PRACTICE

EXAM SELF-CHECK

Exam Success

Before you try to answer, read the exam question and decide:
• What type of business document do I need to write? (letter? fax? report?)
• What is my role (job) in the scenario?
• Who am I writing it for / to?
• What information from the visual material and handwritten notes is essential?

There are two parts to the Writing Test. In Part Two you must write 120–140 words in the form of business correspondence, a short report or a proposal. To help you write, the question will provide visual or graphic material which may have 'handwritten notes' on.

Now answer the exam question. Use this checklist to help you write your report.

Did you ...
- use the correct layout for this type of writing, eg a letter with postal addresses, report with headings? ☐
- use fixed expressions such as I *look forward to hearing from you, It is recommended that* ...? ☐
- use cohesive language and linkers: *Firstly, ... as a result of this* ...? ☐
- use between 120–140 words? ☐
- use an appropriate register, eg formal or informal language? ☐
- include all the key information from the visual information and handwritten notes? ☐
- use sub-headings and paragraphs? ☐
- check carefully for any mistakes at the end? ☐

PART TWO

- You work for a market research company. Your client, a soft drinks company, wants to launch a new flavoured drink. You tested two possible flavours with focus groups. You also asked people to compare normal and diet versions of the two drinks. You have been asked to write a report on your findings and make recommendations to your client.
- Look at the graphs below showing results, on which you have already made some handwritten notes.
- Then using **all** these handwritten notes, write your **report**.
- **Write 120–140 words**.

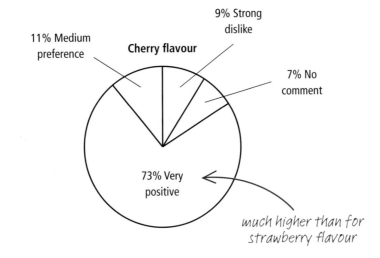

Cherry flavour

9% Strong dislike

11% Medium preference

7% No comment

73% Very positive

much higher than for strawberry flavour

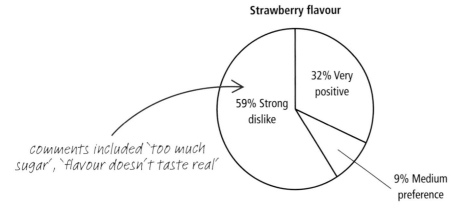

Strawberry flavour

32% Very positive

59% Strong dislike

9% Medium preference

comments included 'too much sugar', 'flavour doesn't taste real'

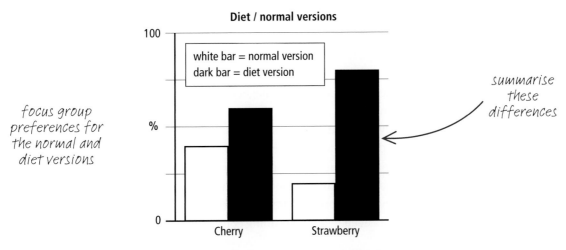

Diet / normal versions

white bar = normal version
dark bar = diet version

focus group preferences for the normal and diet versions

summarise these differences

Cherry   Strawberry

10.1 Management

1 What do you think are the main reasons for Madonna's continued success over the last twenty-five years? Compare your ideas with the article below.

HOW MADONNA MANAGED SUCCESS

Madonna Louise Ciccone Ritchie is a dynamic business woman who has succeeded in the competitive world of the music industry. How has Madonna achieved her success? And why should we care? Well, if we want to succeed in business, we can learn a great deal from the five dimensions of her successful strategy.

Vision

Since high school, Madonna has set herself a clear target: to become the world's number one female performer. If she hadn't set out with this vision, success wouldn't even have been a possibility. Firms too must have a vision of where they want to go and how to get there. (**1**) _____

Understand the industry

Madonna was one of the world's first artists to bring the focus group approach to the music industry. In mid-2005 she partnered with DJ and producer Stuart Price to test tunes (without vocals) in nightclubs around Europe. The reaction of the dancers was filmed and used to determine the tracks for Confessions on a Dance Floor. (**2**) _____

Exploit your competences, address your weaknesses

Another important element in Madonna's success has been her ability to recognise her own competences and weaknesses. Very early on in her career Madonna realised that neither her dancing nor voice were strong enough on their own. She knew that if she teamed up with the right people such as Michael Jackson's manager, Freddie de Mann, she'd fill in the gaps. (**3**) _____

Consistent implementation

Madonna isn't the product of any music company – her success is down to her own sheer hard work. Most of her entertainment interests have been owned or operated by her own companies. Likewise in industry, planning a strategy is easy. (**4**) _____

Continuous renewal

The frequent reinvention of Madonna's style and sound has always reflected an acute awareness of changing styles, social norms and attitudes in a rapidly changing industry. (**5**) _____

2 Choose the best sentence A–F to fill gaps 1–5 in the article. There is one extra sentence.

   A Likewise, if companies or managers renew themselves, they last longer than those who don't.

   B Similarly, companies and managers need to develop the right contacts.

   C But the difficulty for managers is how to implement it.

   D In the same way, managers must also investigate and develop a keen understanding of their client's needs and wants.

   E Similarly, managers who don't set career goals will miss opportunities.

   F Managers need to attend training courses to learn how to manage.

3 Work in pairs. The sentences in exercise 2 all give advice on how to be a successful manager. Think of two more pieces of advice for a manager. Tell the class.

Verb + noun combinations

4 Combine the verbs on the left with the nouns on the right. Draw a line between the words. There may be more than one possibility in some cases.

succeed in	business
plan	success
achieve	weaknesses
set	a great deal
miss	targets
recognise	an understanding
learn	a strategy
develop	opportunities

Now check your answers by finding the combinations in the article and sentences A–F on page 96.

5 Read about a company called MusicToday. Use some of the verbs in exercise 4 to complete this article. Change the form of the verb where necessary.

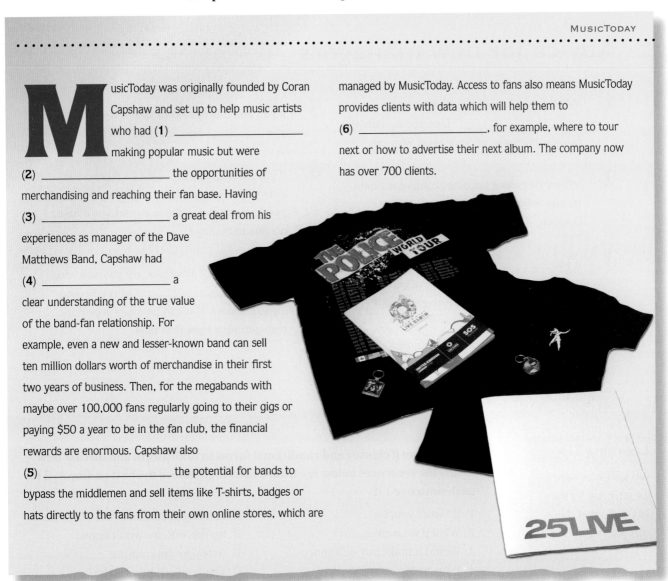

MusicToday was originally founded by Coran Capshaw and set up to help music artists who had (**1**) _____ making popular music but were (**2**) _____ the opportunities of merchandising and reaching their fan base. Having (**3**) _____ a great deal from his experiences as manager of the Dave Matthews Band, Capshaw had (**4**) _____ a clear understanding of the true value of the band-fan relationship. For example, even a new and lesser-known band can sell ten million dollars worth of merchandise in their first two years of business. Then, for the megabands with maybe over 100,000 fans regularly going to their gigs or paying $50 a year to be in the fan club, the financial rewards are enormous. Capshaw also (**5**) _____ the potential for bands to bypass the middlemen and sell items like T-shirts, badges or hats directly to the fans from their own online stores, which are managed by MusicToday. Access to fans also means MusicToday provides clients with data which will help them to (**6**) _____, for example, where to tour next or how to advertise their next album. The company now has over 700 clients.

6 Work in pairs. Cover the article on page 96. Make sentences about Madonna, companies or managers, using each word combination from exercise 4.

Conditionals

1 Read sentences A–E. They are all examples of conditionals. Choose the best sentence to answer each question 1–5.

A If companies or managers renew themselves, they last longer.

B If I were you, I'd team up with a partner.

C If he'd set out with a vision, success would have been more likely.

D If you want personal success in the business world, you can learn a great deal from Madonna.

E If you set yourself career goals, you'll have greater opportunities.

1 Which sentence is about the past? _____ Did the action happen? Yes / No

2 Which sentence describes something that is generally true? _____

3 Which sentence refers to a future possibility? _____

4 Which sentence gives advice? _____

5 In which sentence is *will* replaced by another modal verb? _____

2 Complete this text by writing the verbs in brackets in the correct form to make conditionals. Add a modal verb if necessary.

Advice for new managers

1 Work to your strengths. If you _____ (not do) something, bring someone in on your team who can.

2 When everything becomes routine, it's time to ask, 'What _____ (happen) if we tried it a different way?'

3 If you _____ (want) everyone to like you all the time, you shouldn't have gone into management.

4 Don't give your people targets unless you _____ (know) they can be reached.

5 If you aren't prepared to take risks and fail, you _____ (not succeed).

6 If you _____ (know) the answer to every problem, then you wouldn't need a team. But without a team, you'd have no one to manage!

7 When you make a mistake, ask yourself what you _____ (do) differently if you'd known. This can be more important than getting it right first time.

Learning Tip

When we give advice, we often say *If I were you* instead of *If I was you*.

3 We often use *if* clauses and conditional forms to brainstorm and discuss new ideas. The sentences below are from a meeting. Choose the best ending A–G for each sentence 1–7.

1 If I were you, I'd …

2 What if we were …

3 Would it make any difference …

4 I was wondering if we …

5 What would happen if we …

6 How about if …

7 Unless we …

A to bring in some outside consultants?

B try this out, we won't know.

C redesign the website.

D changed our wholesaler?

E could change our approach.

F the price was lower?

G if we sold it via the website?

Case study

4 You run a management consultancy which gives advice to businesses on how to remain successful and competitive. You have been approached by the music group Soundblaster who would like your consultancy's advice. Study this information about them and list their problems:

MUSIC REVIEW

Soundblaster:
TALK TO THE WORLD

Record label: ANI
Star rating: ★☆☆☆☆

It was always going to be a tough challenge to equal the phenomenally successful *Hear to Believe* but after three years of waiting you would have expected something more original from Soundblaster's third studio album. *Talk to the World* will of course appeal to the band's core fans. It has the same funk guitar sounds and disco rhythms but by the end you feel they are still living in 2003 both in terms of music and appearance …

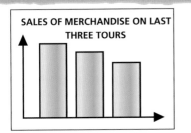

SALES OF MERCHANDISE ON LAST THREE TOURS

CD Sales

2001 Soundblaster I	3.5 million copies	
2003 Hear to believe	5.1 million copies	
2004 Soundblaster live	3.1 million copies	
2007 Talk to the world	2.9 million copies	

5 The band are now planning to record and launch a new CD. They want your consultancy to prepare a report on how they can improve on their success. Hold a brainstorming meeting with two colleagues, with the following agenda:

1 Define a clear target for Soundblaster.
2 How to develop the band's brand.
3 How to develop the band's music and attract new fans.
4 How to increase sales of music and merchandising such as T-shirts, posters, etc.
5 Prepare a presentation of your strategy for the band.

Work in groups of three. Read about your roles and start your meeting. Try to use some of the expressions in exercise 3 on page 98.

Student A: You are an expert in brand management. Look at File 10.1 on page 127.
Student B: You are an expert in market research. Look at File 10.2 on page 132.
Student C: You are an expert in product placement. Look at File 10.3 on page 131.

6 Join another group. Take turns to give your presentations and ask each other questions about your strategy.

A report on a meeting

7 Write a report of what you decided in your meeting and recommend your strategy to the band.

10.2 Solving problems

Problems and solutions

I 🔘 10.1 **Listen to Linda telephoning her manager.**

1 What is she in charge of?
2 What's the main problem?
3 What does she want her manager to do?

2 🔘 10.1 **Listen again and complete the notes on the message pad.**

Linda called from the (1) _____ .
There's a problem. The (2) _____ for the
(3) _____ of the building have arrived but
(4) _____ of them don't fit. They are
(5) _____ centimetres too wide. She thinks
the fault is with the (6) _____ not the
(7) _____ . Please (8) _____
as soon as possible.

3 **Study this flowchart showing ways to solve a problem.**

1	2	3	4	5
What is the problem?	What is one possible solution?	What is another possible solution?	What are the pros and cons of each solution?	What is the best solution?

🔘 10.2 **Roger calls Linda back to discuss possible solutions to the problem with the windows. Listen and answer the five questions in the flowchart above.**

1 _____

2 _____

3 _____

4 Solution A: _____

　Solution B: _____

5 _____

4 🔘 **10.2** Look at the list of expressions below for discussing and solving problems. Listen again and tick the expressions you hear.

Solving problems	
Stating and prioritising	
The main problem is ...	☐
We can worry about ... later.	☐
The main thing is to find a solution.	☐
Let's start by ...	☐
Considering options	
What are our options?	☐
One solution would be to ...	☐
If we do / did ... it will / would ...	☐
My other idea is to ...	☐
It'd have the advantage of ...	☐
On the other hand ... /	
The disadvantage might be ...	☐
One alternative is to ...	☐
Agreeing / Disagreeing	
Good idea. / I agree.	☐
I'm not so sure. / I don't think it'll work.	☐

SPEAKING

Discussing problems

5 Work in pairs. Make a series of telephone calls to each other in order to solve these problems. Follow the flowchart on page 100 and practise using the expressions above.

Problem 1
The new office furniture has arrived but it doesn't fit together. You don't know if it's the fault of the designer or the manufacturer. You need the offices ready by tomorrow.

Problem 2
You want to promote your company more widely without increasing the advertising budget.

Problem 3
You need someone to manage the warehouse. You could either contact a recruitment agency or promote someone within the company.

Managing Projects

1 Here are some word combinations that are often used when managing projects. Decide if you think the phrase could be positive (+) or negative (-) or possibly both (+/-).

out of time (-)   in time ( )   on time ( )   within budget ( )

over budget ( )   under budget ( )   on schedule ( )

behind schedule ( )   ahead of schedule ( )

2 The manager of a music management firm is planning ticket sales and merchandising for a band's next tour. He sends this email to update staff on plans. He has attached a Gantt chart. (This is a management tool often used for planning.) Fill the gaps (1–9) in the email with the words from the box.

> in   behind   over   in   on   in   within   in   ahead

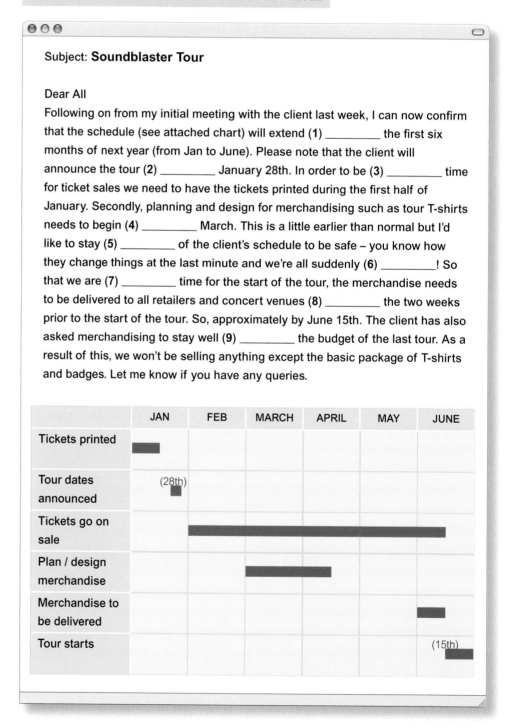

Subject: **Soundblaster Tour**

Dear All

Following on from my initial meeting with the client last week, I can now confirm that the schedule (see attached chart) will extend (**1**) _____ the first six months of next year (from Jan to June). Please note that the client will announce the tour (**2**) _____ January 28th. In order to be (**3**) _____ time for ticket sales we need to have the tickets printed during the first half of January. Secondly, planning and design for merchandising such as tour T-shirts needs to begin (**4**) _____ March. This is a little earlier than normal but I'd like to stay (**5**) _____ of the client's schedule to be safe – you know how they change things at the last minute and we're all suddenly (**6**) _____! So that we are (**7**) _____ time for the start of the tour, the merchandise needs to be delivered to all retailers and concert venues (**8**) _____ the two weeks prior to the start of the tour. So, approximately by June 15th. The client has also asked merchandising to stay well (**9**) _____ the budget of the last tour. As a result of this, we won't be selling anything except the basic package of T-shirts and badges. Let me know if you have any queries.

	JAN	FEB	MARCH	APRIL	MAY	JUNE
Tickets printed	▬					
Tour dates announced	(28th) ▪					
Tickets go on sale		▬▬▬▬▬▬▬▬▬▬▬▬▬▬				
Plan / design merchandise			▬▬▬▬			
Merchandise to be delivered						▬
Tour starts						(15th) ▬

Cause and result

3 The following words and phrases are useful to express the cause and result of actions and decisions. Find four more similar words or phrases in the email on page 102 and write them in.

> further to / _____
>
> so that / _____
>
> due to / because of / _____
>
> therefore / _____

An email

4 Two days later, the manager sends another email to all staff informing them of changes. Complete the email with phrases from exercise 3.

To: All Staff

Subject: Update on Soundblaster tour

(1) _____ my email the other day, the client has informed me of certain changes to the schedule, though we can still start work in January. The tour dates will now be announced a month later and the tour starts two weeks earlier. This is (2) _____ the sales period, which they feel is unnecessarily long, and because two dates have been added to the tour. (3) _____ stay within the planned schedule and not run out of time, we will now need to bring the delivery dates for any merchandising forward by two weeks. The period for planning and design doesn't need to change (4) _____ we have no problems with that. It just means we need to be on schedule for the middle of April (5) _____ we are not late for delivery.

5 Using the information from the email in exercise 4, draw the new schedule on the Gantt chart in exercise 1.

6 Imagine you are the manager of this project. Write another email a week later to all staff.
  - Explain that the tickets will be printed by the end of January.
  - Tell them that the client has increased the merchandise budget so we can include hats and scarves.
  - Thank staff for their patience.

10.3

Listening Test: Part Three

EXAM FORMAT

EXAM PRACTICE

In Part Three of the Listening Test you listen to the longest recording. The recording is usually an interview, conversation or discussion with two or more speakers, or a presentation or report with one speaker.

1 **Look at the instructions for the Listening Test on page 105 and answer the following questions.**

1 How many speakers will you hear?
2 How many questions will you answer?
3 How many possible answers can you choose from in each question?
4 How many times will you hear the interview?

2 **In this part of the exam, the content may include any of the following. Which three do you expect to listen for in this question?**

- advice ☐
- opinions ☐
- criticism ☐
- reports ☐
- descriptions of problems ☐

3 🔘 10.3 **Now listen to the recording and answer the exam questions. After you have listened once, play the recording again.**

Exam Success

- Read the question carefully before listening.
- Before you listen, think about what might be the most likely answer to some of the questions.
- Don't just listen out for facts. Also listen for the speaker's feelings and opinions.
- Use the time between the two listenings to check your answers carefully.
- If there's one question you can't answer, then guess! Don't leave a blank answer.

PART THREE

Questions 1–8

- You will hear an interview on a radio programme with Dede McGee about becoming a manager.
- For each question **1–8**, mark one letter (**A**, **B** or **C**) for the correct answer.
- You will hear the recording twice.

1 What is the first problem that Dede McGee points out?
   - **A** That too many people want to become managers.
   - **B** That many people aren't serious about being a manager.
   - **C** That many people take a management job without thinking it through.

2 The transition to manager can be difficult because
   - **A** you don't solve problems any more.
   - **B** your old colleagues want to spend time with you.
   - **C** you might be in charge of your old colleagues.

3 New managers should avoid
   - **A** socialising with old colleagues.
   - **B** criticising the company.
   - **C** pleasing employees.

4 To become a manager, Dede thinks you
   - **A** should talk to your current manager.
   - **B** shouldn't talk to your manager because you might be seen as a threat.
   - **C** should apply to a new company.

5 Whenever they have the opportunity, potential managers need to
   - **A** take on new responsibilities and attend courses.
   - **B** tell other staff what to do.
   - **C** try and take over their boss's job.

6 Dede McGee says that the main reason for networking is to get
   - **A** a better job.
   - **B** ideas.
   - **C** friends.

7 New managers can become frustrated because
   - **A** they don't have time to get their work done.
   - **B** they spend less time working at a practical level.
   - **C** they spend too much time complaining.

8 Her final piece of advice is to
   - **A** model yourself on your old boss.
   - **B** identify and build on what you are good at.
   - **C** show staff that you will make changes.

Ethical economics

1 The two photos below show the beginning and the end of the process of making coffee. Work in pairs. How many stages can you think of in between to complete the process?

2 These four visual aids refer to the economics of the coffee trade. Read the article on page 107 and write in the missing facts and figures in these visual aids.

Only (1) _____ goes to the grower.

EXPORTS

10% = OTHER

90% = (7) _____

Key facts: Ethiopia
(2) _____ million people in coffee trade
(3) _____ % of GDP
(4) _____ pence = a labourer's pay per day

Coffee Shop Outgoings
Salaries £115,000
(5) _____ £65,000
(6) _____ £20,000
Overheads £80,500

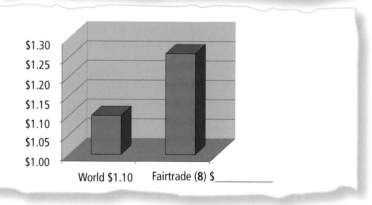

$1.30
$1.25
$1.20
$1.15
$1.10
$1.05
$1.00

World $1.10   Fairtrade (8) $_____

3 Write in the correct letter, A–F, for the missing sentences to complete the text. There is one extra sentence.

A This process alone adds at least 50% to its price.

B Here, coffee production is the staple crop for many millions of growers.

C The only bit controlled in the Fairtrade system is the price a farmer is paid for produce.

D Coffee is the second most traded commodity in the world after oil.

E It guarantees to pay growers a fixed proportion for their coffee, which is above standard market rates.

F Local council taxes add another £25,000 to that.

Coffeenomics:
the true cost of our caffeine addiction

The next time you hand over £3 for your deluxe cappuccino, ask yourself how much the roasted beans that went into that cup really cost. For your average cup of coffee, the producer receives roughly 10p – that's about 3.5%. This **disparity** is causing increasing concern among some **charities** who believe that the excessive profits of coffee shop chains come at the expense of vulnerable coffee producers in countries like Ethiopia, Kenya or Latin America. (**1**) _____ For example, in Ethiopia alone, 15 million people depend on the coffee trade, which constitutes around 50% of the country's **gross domestic product** (GDP) and 90% of its exports. The average wage paid to labourers who pick the beans and work on farms is about 50p a day.

So where do the added costs come from? According to experts, by the time it is consumed by us in our homes or in a coffee shop, the bean may actually **change hands** up to 150 times, each time facing a **mark-up** as it is transported, roasted, packaged and sold. (**2**) _____ Then another 10% in export costs with **freight** and insurance before an importer takes over. Finally, it is sold to us in a coffee shop – and running a coffee shop is not cheap. For example, take your typical coffee shop in a shopping precinct, seating 75 inside and 50 outside. The rent is £65,000 per year plus a service charge of £20,000 a year. (**3**) _____ In other words, even before adding staffing costs and **overheads**, setting aside an amount for redecoration and maintenance on the property, this particular coffee shop needs to sell a minimum of 50,000 coffees a year, or 200 coffees a day. **Factor in** these additional costs and we are probably talking about a **break-even total** of 400 coffees a day.

However, irrespective of how much we end up paying or the reasons why, the reality is that growers themselves see only a tiny proportion of that amount. Organisations like Fairtrade do try to make a difference. (**4**) _____ For example, a farmer selling a pound of Fairtrade Arabica coffee is paid $1.26 compared to the world market price of $1.10 a pound. The Fairtrade price also includes 5¢ which is invested back into community projects. Many shops and coffee bars do now offer Fairtrade coffee to customers alongside their standard offering, but not all of that inflated price goes to the grower. (**5**) _____ After that, mark-ups are determined by the retailers and **middlemen**. That said, at least Fairtrade is one small step that does help farmers around the world get a better price for their products.

Financial and trade terms

4 Match these definitions to the words in bold in the article.

1 People who handle goods between the producer and the retailer. _____
2 A large difference (in price, for example). _____
3 Be bought and sold. _____
4 Cost of heating, lighting and electricity. _____
5 Take items into account to calculate costs. _____
6 The amount needed to pay costs before profit. _____
7 The amount added to the product when it is sold. _____
8 Goods which are transported by ships, planes, lorries, etc. _____
9 The total value of goods and services produced by a country in one year. _____
10 Organisations which help and represent the interests of a group of people in need. _____

The economics of your country

5 Work in small groups and discuss the following questions about each of your countries. If you don't know all the answers to the questions, try to find out for the next lesson and prepare a short presentation.

1 Is there a large disparity between rich and poor in your country?
2 Do you think the disparity between poor and rich countries can be controlled? Should it be controlled?
3 What are some of the biggest charities in your country? Do they have much influence over your government and businesses?
4 What are the most important products and services for your country's GDP?

Articles

1 Write in the missing articles *the, a, an,* or 0 (the zero article) in this text about Fairtrade.

(1) _____ Fairtrade is (2) _____ international certification mark used in 21 countries as (3) _____ marketing initiative to help developing nations. Britain has (4) _____ largest Fairtrade market in (5) _____ world, which has seen (6) _____ amazing increase over the last five years. The organisation is also strong in (7) _____ Netherlands, where Fairtrade first started, and in Switzerland and Scandinavia. Originally started in 1989 as (8) _____ scheme to help poor producers, (9) _____ Fairtrade Foundation was established three years later. Now there are over (10) _____ 550 certified producers representing over one million farmers in 52 countries.

Fairtrade

2 Can you buy these Fairtrade products in your country? Would you buy these products even if they were more expensive? Why? Why not?

3 🔊 **11.1 Listen to an interview with Ian Bretman, the deputy director of the Fairtrade Foundation. Choose the best ending A, B or C for each sentence 1–8.**

1 The Fairtrade Foundation began in
   A 1989.
   B 1990.
   C 1992.

2 When the United States withdrew from the international coffee agreement, the price of coffee decreased by
   A 50%.
   B 0.5%.
   C twenty million.

3 One way Fairtrade helps farmers is by giving advice on how to
   A diversify by growing other crops.
   B produce more coffee.
   C be profitable in a global market.

4 One of Fairtrade's main messages to governments is that
   A trade can be managed more effectively.
   B economic growth is the best strategy.
   C they must invest more in producers.

5 Ian believes that Fairtrade and free trade
   A cannot both exist.
   B can operate together.
   C are basically the same thing.

6 Even though a country may increase its wealth through business, this does not guarantee
   A it can compete internationally.
   B everyone receives the benefits.
   C social justice.

7 If producers are successful, they will also
   A invest in the economy.
   B become the people who buy products.
   C be able to supply more coffee.

8 As well as improving its public image, a Fairtrade company will
   A sell more.
   B attract more talented staff.
   C attract well-informed consumers.

SPEAKING

Giving reasons and benefits

4 **A coffee shop in your town is thinking of selling Fairtrade coffee. However, it is concerned that this may be more expensive.**

Imagine you and your partner work for Fairtrade. You are going to try and convince the coffee shop to use coffee from your producers. Discuss and prepare:
- a list of reasons why the coffee shop should change.
- a list of benefits for the coffee shop, its staff and its customers.

Afterwards, present your ideas to the rest of the class.

11.2 Discussing trends

Alternative energy sources

1 With some types of energy running out, countries are looking at alternative ways of producing energy for the future. To do this will require financial investment. Which of these would you invest your money in? Explain why.

2 Now read the article on the next page about investing in solar power. Choose the best word A, B, C or D to fill the gaps 1–15.

1 A do	B make	C have	D give
2 A of	B in	C by	D for
3 A sector	B company	C department	D division
4 A dollars	B cash	C amounts	D profits
5 A shop	B share	C personally	D publicly
6 A sell	B buy	C invest	D grow
7 A by	B in	C on	D at
8 A report	B charge	C deal	D responsible
9 A concerns	B personality	C problems	D difficulties
10 A than	B as	C so	D more
11 A Although	B Nevertheless	C Despite	D Moreover
12 A ever	B always	C fast	D to
13 A move	B go	C push	D continue
14 A where	B why	C who	D when
15 A begin	B first	C start	D money

'Good greed'

Do you want to know how to (1) _____ money and do your bit for the environment? Investing (2) _____ something that will save the planet is becoming easier as the private (3) _____ begins to step in with powerful, profit-driven solutions for huge world problems. Take energy, for example. More and more investors are now looking to risk huge (4) _____ in alternative energies safe in the knowledge that the world is not safe from carbon emissions.

Solar power is one such case. There are a dozen or so (5) _____ traded companies that manufacture solar materials or systems. And some big-name billion-dollar investors have already rushed to (6) _____ stocks; one producer of high-efficiency solar-power cells, for example, was recently trading (7) _____ the stock market at more than 166 times earnings.

Cautious investors can't forget that a similar optimism was (8) _____ for the **peak** in e-business stocks in the nineties before the **crash**. In the case of solar power, such (9) _____ are well-founded because solar energy has one big economic problem: it currently costs roughly twice (10) _____ much per kilowatt-hour as power from the grid.

(11) _____, events are changing in a way that may encourage all investors. First, of course, there are **rising** petroleum prices and no one really believes the cost of natural gas will (12) _____ **go down** again. Secondly, even as traditional energy prices begin to **soar**, solar costs are expected to (13) _____ their **descent**. The cost of a solar kilowatt-hour has **declined** from 47 cents in 1990 to around 21 cents today, (14) _____ it has **remained stable**. The third force is government subsidies. In the USA, for example, Uncle Sam now gives a 30% tax credit to businesses that use solar energy – and that's just the (15) _____, with much more still to come.

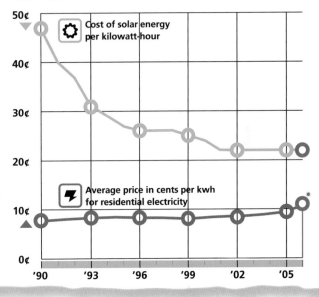

3 What does the graph tell you about solar energy? Do you think it's a good moment to invest?

Describing trends

4 In the last two paragraphs of the article there are eight words or pairs of words in bold that describe trends. Complete this table with the words and write if the word is a verb (v), noun (n) or adjective (a).

→	→	↘	～↗
to increase (v) increase (n) (1) _____ to go up (v) (2) _____ ascend (v) ascent (n) (3) _____	level out (v) (4) _____	to decrease (v) decrease (n) to fall (v) fall (n) (5) _____ (6) _____ (7) _____ (8) _____	fluctuate (v) fluctuation (n)

Do you know any more words or expressions to describe trends? Add them to the table.

Reasons for trends

1 🎧 11.2 **Listen to five investors giving advice about different types of energy. In each case, they describe an overall trend. Decide which trend, A–F, is being described and write the number of the speaker. There is one extra trend shown.**

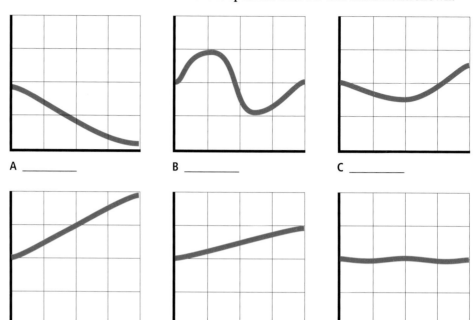

A _____   B _____   C _____

D _____   E _____   F _____

2 🎧 11.2 **Listen to the five speakers again and write in the missing words.**

1 ... is probably a good long-term investment _____ its growth has been slow but fairly consistent ...

2 It's all a bit up and down _____ _____ _____ _____ _____ some governments are saying now is the time to look for alternative energies ...

3 _____ _____ _____ putting your money in oil companies is that quite a few are also developing environmentally-friendly fuels ...

4 Anyway, _____ _____ _____ _____ governments suddenly realising for at least the next century we won't be able to get enough energy from natural sources, nuclear will probably ...

5 I don't predict they're going to see much change in the near future, either, _____ it's going to be slow to develop.

Discussing trends

3 **Work in pairs. What have been the overall trends for the following in your country?**

- house prices
- number of older and younger members of the population
- results in schools
- unemployment
- immigration
- interest rates

Now give reasons for these trends using the words and expressions in exercise 2.

I think house prices have risen because there are more single people and as a result of some people buying second homes ...

A proposal

4 Read the information below about Sungreen Power. Make a list of reasons for and against investing in the company.

PRESS RELEASE

Sungreen Power Announces 190 Million Euro Sales Agreement with Mainline Energy

As from today, we are pleased to announce that Sungreen Power will supply Mainline Energy with solar technology for the next five years …

Sungreen POWER COMPANY

Corporate Profile

Sungreen Power, founded in 1995, develops, manufactures and sells solar panels that provide reliable and environmentally clean electric power throughout the world. The Company expects to exploit its technology to produce innovative and original products, to reduce manufacturing costs through its new silicon-saving technology, and to manufacture for the global market …

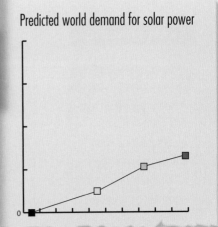

Predicted world demand for solar power

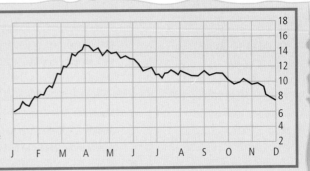

Sungreen Power Stock Price Takes a Fall

Sungreen's stock price has fallen by about half since it hit a high of $15.50 earlier in the year. This comes as a result of industry concerns that a shortage of silicon – the material needed to make solar cells – will hurt manufacturers. However, many analysts describe this as a short-term problem since Sungreen specialises in a technology which aims to reduce the amount of silicon needed.

5 Imagine you are an investment advisor. One of your clients is interested in investing in environmentally-friendly businesses and has heard about Sungreen Power. He thinks the company might be a good investment and has asked for your advice. Write a proposal (120–140 words) to explain:

- the current pros and cons of the investment
- if you think it is a good investment

This list of expressions will help you.

Making a proposal
Introducing the proposal
In response to your enquiry about …
At present the company seems to be performing (well / badly) …
Comparing pros and cons
On the one hand … but on the other …
One advantage / disadvantage is that …
One other thing to consider is …
Balancing and concluding
Despite … I would still suggest that …
Overall, I would strongly recommend that …
The fact that … makes this a good / poor investment opportunity.

11.3

Reading Test: Part Three

There are five parts to the Reading Test. In this Exam spotlight you will look at Part Three. It is always one text, such as an article from a newspaper or business advice of about 500 words. You have to answer six multiple choice questions with four answers to choose from.

Read the Exam Success Box, then answer the exam questions.

Exam Success

• Read the whole text first followed by the questions. And then start to answer.
• The questions normally test if you understand the overall meaning – not simply one word.
• Don't be worried if there are some words you don't know.

PART THREE
Questions 1–6

• Read the article about the importance of writing a covering letter when applying for a job, and answer the questions on the opposite page.
• For each question **1–6**, mark one letter (**A**, **B**, **C** or **D**).

Selling yourself on paper: how to write a covering letter

A good covering letter for a new job is like a firm handshake. It's a good way to be remembered and to say 'choose me'! It accompanies your CV and is just as important. 'A covering letter is read before a CV, so make sure that it grabs the reader's attention,' says Paul Laurie, the operations manager at the employment consultancy Manpower. Many employers don't even bother to read the CV if the letter has poor spelling and punctuation, forgets to include contact details or omits reference to what the job is. These apparently are all common reasons for not even making the interview stage. The other point to note is that it isn't just an optional extra. Even if the advert only requires you to email your CV, you need to introduce why your CV is there and what you stand for. It should set the scene and make the reader want to open the attachment.

Many applicants begin with the rather anonymous Dear Sir or Madam, but if the job advertisement doesn't name a contact, call human resources to find out who will be shortlisting applications. The sooner you get on personal terms with the head of human resources, the better. Laurie also advises you to 'keep it punchy'. This means that three or four paragraphs should be sufficient to convey your motivation, experience and personality. It isn't replacing your CV but summarises your suitability for a role by matching your experience to the job advertised. This doesn't mean crossing that line between truth and fiction. 'There is selling yourself and then highlighting what you have done,' Laurie says. 'Avoid statements such as "I am the ideal candidate", for example, in favour of "I believe I have the skills and experience that make me a strong candidate."'

Of course, you might not be replying to a job advert but simply writing a speculative application. Perhaps you recently read something in the trade press or met someone from a firm at a networking event? If so, give a clear reason for writing and this will tell the company that you have been doing your homework. Recruiters are always impressed by any evidence of research into their company's goals, achievements and vision. Also, with this speculative application letter, don't be discouraged if you don't get a job straight away. There may not be a job to suit you at the time of writing but most HR managers will keep impressive letters and CVs on file. It's also worth making a follow-up call a month or so later to remind them that you exist.

More and more covering application letters are now actually sent in the form of emails. But don't see the email as a shortcut. A good email requires just as much patience as a legible handwritten letter. You can also make an email work harder by writing a subject line with your key point, for example 'Engineering Graduate'. And as with letters, don't point out any weaknesses and then attempt to justify yourself – you're giving reasons to interview you, not delete you. Finally, sign off with confidence and ask for an interview. Ending with 'I'll expect your call' sounds overly confident whereas writing that you expect to meet to discuss the role sounds professional.

1 In the first paragraph, the writer recommends that a covering letter should
   A include the words 'choose me'.
   B include a CV.
   C make the reader look at your CV.
   D not include as much information as the CV.

2 According to the writer, not all covering letters
   A are needed.
   B include the name of the sender.
   C are attached to emails.
   D explain their purpose.

3 What are the reasons for telephoning the company?
   A It's more effective than writing a letter.
   B So you get to know who the contact person is.
   C To find out what kind of job vacancies they have.
   D To find out what kind of applications they prefer.

4 According to the writer, one mistake people make is to
   A exaggerate about themselves.
   B say they are better than others.
   C lie about their experience.
   D apply for unadvertised jobs.

5 What does the writer say about speculative letters?
   A Don't expect to get a reply.
   B Ask to be kept on file if there aren't currently any vacancies.
   C Try to hand deliver them to the person in charge.
   D Show that you have studied the company.

6 What advice does the writer give about applications by email?
   A Employers prefer them.
   B Make a copy in case it's deleted.
   C Mention areas you still intend to work on.
   D The same guidelines apply as for the traditional letter.

12.1

Business law

A colour problem

1 Here are the two logos of rival mobile phone operators. What legal problem do you think might occur between them?

2 🔘 12.1 Listen to a news programme about the problem in exercise 1. A journalist has prepared notes on the case. Write in the missing words.

> Galacall announced that it may take legal proceedings over a series of
> (1) _____ run by its rival Frontline.
> It may sue the company over its use of the colour purple on
> (2) _____ worn by sales staff.
> This is a similar case to that of Orange and easyMobile and the argument over the use of
> the colour (3) _____ in both companies' trademarks.
> Another example is when BP took out litigation against an Irish
> (4) _____ over its petrol stations and the fact they
> wanted to paint them (5) _____.
> As well as colour, a company trademark can have the rights over the
> (6) _____ of a logo or brand.
> Galacall will win in court if the prosecution can prove their
> (7) _____ is damaged by confusing
> (8) _____.

Legal terms

Learning Tip

Use a good dictionary to help you.

3 Match these legal words to their definitions A–J. Some appear in the notes in exercise 2.

0 sue ___D___
1 prosecute _____
2 trademark _____
3 court _____
4 lawyer _____
5 case _____
6 rights _____
7 judge _____
8 defence _____
9 litigation _____

A Name or symbol on a product which means it cannot be used by another producer.

B Legal matter that is decided in court.

C The process of taking a case to court.

D Make a legal case against someone and claim for money.

E What you are legally allowed to do.

F The place where legal cases are heard.

G The person who gives legal advice and represents a person in court.

H The person in charge of a court who makes legal decisions.

I Try to prove someone is guilty.

J The case to prove someone is innocent.

Colourful cases

4 Read three articles about companies and their trademarks. Which article (A, B or C) does each of these statements 1–7 refer to?

1 The case was over the colour of the premises. _____
2 The company is unlikely to take members of the public to court. _____
3 The company already used the colour on its other brands. _____
4 The company has not yet started any kind of litigation. _____
5 Only part of the company could be prosecuted. _____
6 The rights of a company in another country were affected. _____
7 The company would like to control how its brand is used. _____

A

ORANGE TO SUE OVER COLOUR

The mobile operator Orange may be taking easyMobile to court over trademarks. The problem comes from the easyMobile choice of colour. The operator has followed the easyGroup trademark branding and used orange. The two mobile companies have been in litigation since the launch of easyMobile was announced, but Orange has said that the talks failed to resolve the issues and the two operators will see each other in court. Joel Barry, partner with legal firm Olswang, said that the case will be the first in the UK to see a legal battle over a corporate colour.

B

NO GOOGLING, PLEASE

Internet search giant Google has said it intends to stop the use of its name as a generic verb, saying that phrases such as 'to google' somebody or something are potentially damaging to its brand. A spokeswoman for Google said: 'We think it's important to make the distinction between using the word Google to describe using Google to search the Internet and using the word Google to generally describe searching the Internet. There are some serious trademark issues.' But Dr Julie Coleman, an authority on linguistics from the University of Leicester, says that once new words enter into common usage it is impossible to stop their use. 'Google can't possibly stop the spread of the verb,' said Coleman. 'Normal people are using it in normal conversation and in writing and they aren't likely to face legal proceedings.'

C

GOING GREEN

In 1996, the Irish company Tedcastles Oil Products, or TOP, decided to modernise its petrol stations by painting them green. They felt the colour green would reflect the company's traditional Irish values. The company's subsidiary in Northern Ireland also painted its stations green. However, these stations came under United Kingdom law. In June 1991 the British oil company BP had applied for a trademark to protect the green colour of its service stations and so it quickly set about taking action against TOP, even though TOP's green was darker ...

5 Discuss each of the cases together.

- How important do you think a trademark is? Do you think it affects what people buy?
- What do you think of the points of view of Orange, Google and BP? Do you agree with them?

Indirect questions and tags

1 🔘 **12.1 Listen to the news programme from exercise 2 on page 116 again. Re-write the direct questions below as indirect questions and tags.**

0 How serious is Galacall about this?

I was wondering how serious _Galacall is about this_ ?

1 Do they only have a case against a company which infringes the trademark by using a similar name?

They only have a case against a company which infringes the trademark by using a similar name, _____?

2 Can you use the same colour as long as your product is different?

Do you think _____ as long as your product is different?

3 Is there anything else you can buy the rights on?

Can you tell me if _____ you can buy the rights on?

4 What do you think the outcome will be if it ever gets to court?

I'd like to know what _____ if it ever gets to court.

2 Why do you think the speaker uses indirect questions and tags?

3 Read these questions and comments from a BEC Vantage Speaking Test. Find the mistake in each one. Check for word order, an incorrect word or a missing word.

1 Do you think will business become more global in the future?

2 I was wondering you think the most important thing is when setting up a new business.

3 Good marketing is more important than a good product, is it?

4 In the future, people will reduce how much they travel by plane, won't it?

5 Do you think can employees work as well from home as from an office?

6 I'd like to ask you what are your plans for your future career?

7 What kinds of work experience you think would help students at business school?

8 You've studied English for three years, aren't you?

4 Work in pairs. Take turns to ask and answer the questions in exercise 3.

The BEC Vantage speaking game

5 Prepare and practise for asking and answering questions in the BEC Speaking Test by playing this game.

- Work in groups of three or four.
- You will each need two counters, for example a small coin.
- Place one counter on the START square on the outer track, and the second counter on any square on the inner track – it doesn't matter which one.
- Each player takes turns to roll the dice.
- Move both counters clockwise according to the number of squares on the dice.
- When you land on a square on the outer track you must ask any player of your choice a question about the topic written on that square. Your question must begin with the words shown on the square on the inner track.
- A FREE QUESTION square means you can choose any topic to ask about.
- If the rest of the players think a speaker made a mistake when asking a question, he or she misses a go.

| websites | meeting skills | applying for a job | FREE QUESTION | ambitions |

setting up a new business				dress code
recruitment	I'd like to know	Can you tell me	Why	holidays
team building	Where		Do you think	customers
FREE QUESTION	Who		Is	shopping / prices
giving presentations	How		What	emailing
forms of advertising	What		How	FREE QUESTION
food and drink	Do		Can	market research
training / education	Does		What do you think	management skills
ways of working	Could you tell me	I was wondering	Are	the latest news
home or country				hotels / travel
START FINISH	online business	FREE QUESTION	selling	qualifications

12.2

Handling questions

Difficult questions

1 Discuss why people might ask questions in the following situations.

A A customer wants to return an item.

B An employee receives a pay cheque at the end of the month.

C A student gets poor marks for a business exam.

D A manager discovers an employee has been sending emails to friends.

E A public relations manager is explaining a faulty product to journalists at a press conference.

2 🔘 12.2 Listen to five conversations. Match the situations A–E in exercise 1 to conversations 1–5.

Conversation 1: _____

Conversation 2: _____

Conversation 3: _____

Conversation 4: _____

Conversation 5: _____

3 🔘 12.2 Listen again and match the questions 1–6 to the responses A–F.

1 What else was I supposed to write?

2 Do you have any ideas about what caused the problem?

3 How soon will these items be back on the shelves?

4 Why hasn't it been included?

5 Can I exchange it for another one?

6 You do know our policy with regard to this, don't you?

A I just need to check with someone first.

B Sorry, I don't follow you.

C I'm afraid I'm unable to answer that at the moment.

D Can you explain what you mean?

E Let me get back to you on that.

F That's a very good question.

4 Write the responses A–F from exercise 3 into this language summary.

Handling questions
Delaying your answer
Do you mind if I answer that at the end?
(1) _____
(2) _____
(3) _____
I'd like to come back to that point later on, if that's OK.
Commenting on the question
(4) _____
Thank you for asking that.
Asking for further explanation or repetition
Sorry, I didn't understand the question.
(5) _____
Sorry, I didn't hear you. / catch that.
(6) _____
Could you repeat that? / say that again?

SPEAKING

Responding to questions

5 How would you respond to a question in the following situations?

1 A job interviewer asks you a very complicated question. You need him to repeat it.

2 A journalist telephones you to ask about a possible new joint venture between you and another company. It is true but the final contract hasn't been agreed yet.

3 You're a politician and an angry member of the public asks you why you have increased the rate of tax for homeowners.

4 It's your first day at a banking call centre. A customer calls and asks about taking out a $5,000 loan but wants a different interest rate to the one advertised.

5 Someone interrupts you in the middle of trying to explain a complicated new system.

6 You are a PR representative for a pharmaceutical company. A new skincare product has given some customers red spots on their faces. You are answering questions at a press conference.

6 Think of a question for each of the situations in exercise 5. Then work in pairs and take turns to ask your question and give an appropriate response.

Press releases

1 Read the 'How to ...' article on writing press releases and answer the following
questions.

1 Why do people write press releases?
2 When will newspapers or broadcasters use your news?
3 What is the advantage of a press release over normal advertising?

How to ... write a press release

You may think that writing press releases only works when you have important
news to share or company announcements to make but that is wrong! You can
write and submit press releases which will get published in newspapers or
broadcast on TV or radio at any time if you give an interesting slant to what
you are submitting. Here are some interesting ideas to help get your press
release picked up by the media:

• Write a story about how your business helps your community or solves a
  problem for local people.
• Write a press release if your company has raised money for charity.
• Tell your personal story: maybe you set up your business from nothing or
  you are a local success story.
• Relate your story to what is happening today – watch the news, check out
  what the 'hot topics' are and find a way to 'spin' a story from that.
• Make sure the press release doesn't sound like an advertisement. The idea is
  that consumers will think they are reading a news story rather than being
  sold something.

2 A local newspaper has received four press releases this morning. According to the
article above, which release (A–D) isn't a good one? Tell your partner why.

A

As many of you are aware, environmental concerns are now
at the front of everyone's minds. But while many companies
say they are concerned, we at Beavis and Son are taking this
very seriously, and we are therefore pleased to announce our
new 'buy a bag for the Amazon' scheme. Unlike most stores,
where you get a free plastic bag which you then throw away,
at Beavis and Son we will sell you a strong reusable bag, with
the cost going to a charity which saves the rainforests of the
Amazon ...

B

It is always good to hear of a local success story and we
are delighted that Rainer's Furnishings are now going
global with the opening of their first ever factory
overseas. The company will be taking over a firm based
in Poznan in Poland and re-equipping the factory there.
Contrary to recent suggestions that the company may
use this as an opportunity to reduce the size of its local
factory, the company's managing director Malcolm
Storey was able to confirm with staff at a recent meeting
that this was not a step towards downsizing or cost-
cutting but expansion ...

C

I am writing to inform your readers of our spring
sale starting next week. All clothing items will
have discounts saving you as much as 20% ...

D

While we are sad to see her go, we are celebrating the retirement
of our founder Roselyn Cooper-Hennes. Roselyn is handing over
the running of her company to her two sons, Richard and Mark,
exactly thirty years after founding the company. As many local
people will know, Roselyn was an active member of the local
council. Perhaps they don't know, however, that Roselyn actually
started the business from a small kitchen in a tiny house ...

3 Match the press release (A, B, C or D) to the statements below.

This press release ...
1 is more like an advertisement. _____
2 starts to tell a story. _____
3 is about raising money for charity. _____
4 refers to a 'hot topic'. _____
5 describes a recent achievement. _____
6 explains a benefit to the customer. _____
7 refers to some bad publicity. _____

4 Work in groups of three. You are the editors of the newspaper. This week there is only space for one of these press releases. Discuss which one to use.

5 Look at the underlined phrases in the four press releases and write them next to these functions.

Introduces the news   _____
                                   _____
Refers to reader's knowledge   _____
                                   _____
Announces good news   _____
                                   _____
                                   _____
Handles bad news   _____
                                   _____

A press release

6 Write a press release using the information below.

You work in the press office for a local theatre called the Everyman. The manager has just sent you this email. He wants a press release to be sent to the editor of the local paper. Use the email and the handwritten notes you have already made. Try to use some of the expressions in exercise 5. Send your press release in the form of a letter to the editor.

• Recent reports in the press that the theatre might be closing are totally untrue
• The next musical stars the TV actor Rene Travis
• Café will also be open during the day selling snacks and sandwich lunches — people shopping will be interested
• There will be cabaret nights in the café
• Money for the new café was raised by the organisation 'Friends of the Everyman' and a grant from the local council

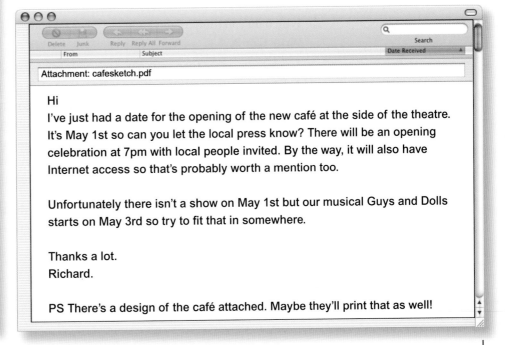

Attachment: cafesketch.pdf

Hi
I've just had a date for the opening of the new café at the side of the theatre. It's May 1st so can you let the local press know? There will be an opening celebration at 7pm with local people invited. By the way, it will also have Internet access so that's probably worth a mention too.

Unfortunately there isn't a show on May 1st but our musical Guys and Dolls starts on May 3rd so try to fit that in somewhere.

Thanks a lot.
Richard.

PS There's a design of the café attached. Maybe they'll print that as well!

12.3

Speaking Test: Part Three

In this Exam spotlight you will look at Part Three of the Speaking Test. This final part is a two-way conversation between the candidates and then the examiner also joins in the discussion at the end. It lasts about five minutes. Normally there are two candidates in the Speaking Test. However, there could be three candidates. In this case, you will all discuss the topics together. Note that you get extra time if there is an extra candidate.

Exam Success

Take your time to read and understand the topic before you start speaking.

1 Write a phrase you could use for each of the following during the discussion.

Express an opinion: _____

Compare and contrast information: _____

Ask the other person for their opinion: _____

Ask for clarification or repetition: _____

Agree: _____

Disagree: _____

Compare your ideas with a partner and the list of expressions on page 133.

2 **Which do you think is good advice (G) or bad advice (B) for this part of the exam? Write G or B.**

1 Try to say more than your partner and speak for most of the time. (   )
2 Encourage your partner to speak by asking, 'What do you think?' (   )
3 Listen to your partner and respond to his / her comment. (   )
4 Ignore what your partner says and concentrate on saying what you think. (   )
5 Discuss the situation on the Task Sheet and comment on the points listed. (   )
6 Change the topic for discussion if you think it isn't interesting. (   )
7 If possible, agree with the other candidate and reach a conclusion. (   )

3 **Work in pairs or groups of three. Discuss each of the topics on the next page. Spend 3–5 minutes on each.**

Topic 1

Your company is attending a sales conference in Dubai for the first time.
You have been asked to help with preparations for the trip.
Discuss the situation together and decide:
- what kind of travel and hotel arrangements you will need to make
- what kind of free time entertainments delegates will be interested in

Topic 2

Your company is looking for a new head of Human Resources.
You have been asked to help select the candidate.
Discuss the situation together and decide:
- what experience and skills you will look for in applicants
- what kind of package (perks, benefits) you can offer the person in addition to a basic starting salary

Topic 3

Your company is going to launch a new range of stationery and office equipment.
You have been asked to help with promotion.
Discuss the situation together and decide:
- some of the best ways to promote the product
- the advantages and disadvantages of TV advertising

Topic 4

Your company is considering ways of becoming more environmentally friendly.
You have been asked to help implement some of these ways.
Discuss the situation together and decide:
- what kind of policies on recycling you could introduce into your offices
- ways of encouraging employees to reduce how much they use their cars for commuting

Topic 5

Your training department is thinking of introducing more distance and online training.
You have been asked to consider if this is possible.
Discuss the situation together and decide:
- what the advantages of this kind of training will be for employees
- if it is possible for courses in meetings and presentation skills to be delivered online

MODULE 2

File 2.1 Student A

1 distribution centre: place where goods are sent out to be sold
2 warehouse: place where goods are stored
3 holding company: company which controls others with the largest stake (over 51%)
4 call centre: place where employees give information to customers by telephone
5 plant: factory with industrial machinery

MODULE 3

File 3.1 Student A

You find this correspondence on your desk. Make changes to the schedule in exercise 7 and then confirm details with your partner.

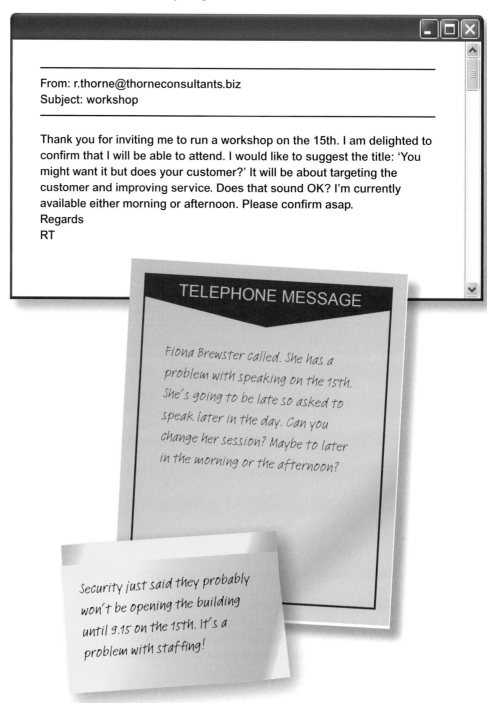

From: r.thorne@thorneconsultants.biz
Subject: workshop

Thank you for inviting me to run a workshop on the 15th. I am delighted to confirm that I will be able to attend. I would like to suggest the title: 'You might want it but does your customer?' It will be about targeting the customer and improving service. Does that sound OK? I'm currently available either morning or afternoon. Please confirm asap.
Regards
RT

TELEPHONE MESSAGE

Fiona Brewster called. She has a problem with speaking on the 15th. She's going to be late so asked to speak later in the day. Can you change her session? Maybe to later in the morning or the afternoon?

Security just said they probably won't be opening the building until 9.15 on the 15th. It's a problem with staffing!

File 3.3 Student A

Your name is Andrzej Welanetz. You telephone Kirsten at Business Circle Conferencing. Request details of the next course on telephone skills and ask them to be sent by email (give your email address). Confirm that you will want to send five members of your staff on this course and find out what discounts can be given on group bookings.

MODULE 9

File 9.1 Student A

Call 1
- Your surname is Jingshan.
- You telephone customer care at your bank.
- Your account number is HIE364 4756.
- You paid in $3,760 last month but it doesn't appear on your statement.
- Your number is 980 765 55 44.

Call 2
Now you are Mr Vathone's secretary. He is unavailable. Find out what the caller wants and find a suitable time for Mr Vathone to call back. Complete this message form.

MODULE 10

File 10.1 Student A

You are an expert in brand management. During the meeting suggest the following possibilities for developing the brand.
- Modernise the band's logo.
- Use their songs on TV commercials or in a film.
- Launch a range of aftershave or perfume called Soundblaster and include this smell inside the CDs.
- Other?

Module 1 *Present tenses*

Present simple
Use this form to talk about:
(1) routine activities: *I normally start work at 9am.*
(2) general facts: *He works for a company in Spain.*

Present continuous
Use this form to talk about:
(1) an activity taking place at or around the time of speaking: *We're doing some consultancy for them at the moment.*
(2) a changing trend or situation: *Interest in our new range is growing faster than even we anticipated.*

Present perfect
Use this form to talk about tasks that started in the past and which continue in the present: *I've sent off half the packages.*
Use it to say what the result of the action is: *I've done everything!*

Present perfect continuous
When talking about the present, use this form to describe an activity that started in the past and continues in the present: *Michael has been working from home for quite a few months.*
We often use it to emphasise the activity or say how long it has taken: *I've been opening boxes for over three hours now!*

Also see Module 2 Grammar Reference for more uses.

(1) We don't usually write 'state' verbs such as *be, need, like, understand* in a continuous form.
(2) Verbs such as *live* and *work* can appear in the present perfect or present perfect continuous form with little change to meaning: *Sandra's worked in customer services since we opened. / Sandra's been working in customer services since we opened.*

Module 2 *Past tenses*

Past simple
Use this form to talk about finished actions in the past: *She started with Xerox in 2001.*

The time / year in the past is often stated or understood, eg *in 2001, yesterday, two years ago.*

Present perfect
Use this form to:
(1) link a present situation to a starting point in the past: *They've worked for Xerox since 2001.*
(2) talk about a past action without saying when it happened (eg an experience): *Have you ever been to a trade fair?*

Present perfect continuous
Use this form to describe a present action that started in the past and is still continuing: *I've been working here since 2001.*

Also see Module 1 Grammar Reference for more uses.

Since and *for*
Since refers to a point in time: *since 2001, since yesterday.*
For refers to a period of time: *for three years, for a day.*

Past continuous
Use this tense to talk about a 'background action': *I was thinking about the problem when my colleague came up with a solution.* This is sometimes an action which is interrupted.

Past perfect
Use the past perfect for an action that happened before another: *He'd cancelled the meeting before we arrived.*

Module 3 Will *and future reference*

Will
Use *will* to:
(1) promise action: *We'll check that for you straight away.*
(2) make a prediction about the future: *They'll probably call later on. / It's unlikely that we'll hear from them.*
(3) announce an unplanned decision:
A: *I'm afraid Rachel's train is delayed.*
B: *OK. I'll go and talk to her visitors.*

To be going to + verb
Use this structure to:
(1) state a pre-planned decision: *I spoke to Rachel earlier. She's delayed so I'm going to talk to her visitors.*
(2) state an intention: *I'm going to apply for a job with them.*

Present simple
Use the present simple for regular timetabled events: *The plane to Paris leaves at nine.*

Present continuous
Use the present continuous for describing future planned arrangements: *We're meeting at three o'clock on Tuesday.*

Also see Module 1 Grammar Reference for more uses.

Future continuous
Use the future continuous as an alternative to the present continuous to refer to future planned arrangements: *The visitors will be arriving at three.*

Future perfect
Use the future perfect to say that something will end before a certain time: *We'll have finished by the time they arrive.*

Module 4 *Modal verbs*

Possibility and ability
The company can / could argue all the information was provided.
Sorry, we can't make it tonight.
The speaker couldn't get here on time.

Obligation and necessity
All advertisers must look at what they are saying.
I mustn't forget my appointment at two.
You have to show your security card at reception.

Lack of obligation and necessity
You didn't have to work late. Why did you?
You needn't do any more on this. I'll finish it.
You don't need to tell them. I'll give them a call.

Giving advice
I think you should tell him about your new job.
We shouldn't invest in that company.

Criticism
They shouldn't have come if they weren't interested.
She ought to have said something about leaving a month ago.

Deduction

He's late. He must be stuck in traffic.
The flight must have been delayed.
The company can't be doing very well. They are making staff redundant.
Richard couldn't have done well at the interview.

Module 5 Reporting

When we report what someone said (direct speech), we often use reported speech:

Direct speech: *'I disagree with the general opinion.'*

Reported speech: *The chairperson said he disagreed with the general opinion.*

We often change the verb tense by moving it into the past when we use reported speech. This table shows some typical changes.

Direct speech	Reported speech
Present simple *'I agree.'*	Past simple *He said he agreed.*
Present continuous *'We are considering your idea.'*	Past continuous *They said they were considering his idea.*
Present perfect *'The price has gone up again.'*	Past perfect *The newsreader said the price had gone up again.*
Past simple *'I told him to see me about the problem.'*	Past perfect *She said she had told him to see her about the problem.*
Can *'I can't come.'*	Could *She said she couldn't come.*
Will *'I'll increase the offer.'*	Would *He said he'd increase the offer.*

Pronouns and adverbs of time

These may change in reported speech:
'I saw you yesterday.' → *He said he'd seen her the day before.*

Say and tell

When we report using *tell* an object is required:
Peter said that he would be late.
Peter told his boss that he would be late.

Other reporting verbs: *argued, called, apologised, agreed, concluded*

Reporting questions

Yes / No questions: *'Is Jan arriving today?'* → *He asked if Jan was arriving today.*

Open questions: *'Why isn't Jan arriving today?* → *He asked why Jan wasn't arriving today.*

Module 6 Passives

Use the passive form when:
(1) we do not know who the person (or agent) is: *This message was left on my desk.*
(2) the person (or agent) is obvious or not important: *The prototype will be tested again tomorrow.*

Form the passive with the verb *to be* and the past participle of the main verb as shown below:

	Active	Passive
Present simple	*We pack the goods.*	*The goods are packed.*
Present perfect	*300 customers have called us.*	*We've been called by 300 customers.*
Past simple	*I founded the company in 1995.*	*The company was founded in 1995.*
Will (future)	*My colleague will speak to you.*	*You will be spoken to by my colleague.*
Present infinitive	*Police are to look into the case.*	*The case is to be looked into.*
It + passive	*The board hopes he will stay on.*	*It is hoped he will stay on.*
Modal	*We can give them more time.*	*They can be given more time.*

Common uses of the passive in business
(1) For describing processes
All letters are placed in this tray for delivery.
The raw materials are left here for production.
(2) For reporting formal decisions / results
It is reported that the figures will be reviewed again in a month.
It was concluded that over half the people questioned wouldn't buy the product.

Module 7 Comparatives and superlatives

Form a comparative or superlative from one-syllable (and some two-syllable) adjectives by adding *-er / -est*:
It was a strange invention.
It was stranger than her last invention.
It was the strangest invention.

For longer adjectives put *more / the most* (or *less / the least*) before the adjective:
It was expensive.
It was more expensive than I'd expected.
It was the most expensive in the shop.

Note these irregular adjectives:
good – better – best
bad – worse - worst

To show two things are equal or similar use *as* + adjective + *as*:
The new version isn't as good as the previous one.

Module 8 -ing *form and infinitive*

Use the -*ing* form after a verb + preposition:
She's working on fixing the problem.
Have you thought of moving into sales?
I'm interested in seeing your plan for this.

Some verbs are always followed by the -*ing* form.
These verbs include *consider, delay, dislike, enjoy, mind, postpone, practise, recommend, suggest*:

Have you considered changing the colour?
Would you mind waiting?
Let's postpone training everyone until next month.

Some verbs are always followed by the infinitive.
These verbs include *afford, arrange, decide, manage, want*:
We can't afford to do this.
Shall we arrange to meet again in an hour?
Do you want to take this course?

Some verbs can be followed by the -*ing* form and infinitive.
These verbs include *advise, propose, begin, continue, like, prefer*:
We advise you to take two weeks off.
We advise taking two weeks off.

There may be a big difference in meaning with some verbs. For example:
(1) *I stopped working there years ago.*
(2) *I stopped to work on this new project.*
Sentence 1 describes a finished action. Sentence 2 describes an interrupted action.

There may be little or no difference in meaning with others. For example:
We prefer to stay at home during the week.
We prefer staying at home during the week.

Module 9 *Relative clauses*

Use the following adverbs or pronouns in relative clauses: *when* (time), *where* (place), *why* (reason), *which* (things), *who* (person), *whose* (possession).

Defining relative clauses add extra and necessary information:
The factory which is in Poland needs a refit.

(The company has more than one factory so the speaker defines it as the one in Poland.)

You can replace the pronouns *who* and *which* with the pronoun *that*:
The factory that is in Poland needs a refit.

Non-defining relative clauses add extra but unnecessary information:
The factory, which is in Poland, needs a refit.

(The company only has one factory so the speaker adds information about the country it is in for interest.)

Put commas at the beginning and end of the non-defining relative clause.

Module 10 *Conditionals*

Use conditionals in the following ways:

General truth
If + present simple → present simple
If you work hard in this business, you succeed.

Possibility/likelihood
If + present simple → *will* ('*ll*) + verb
If you leave now, you'll probably make it on time.

Giving advice
If + past simple → *would* ('*d*) + verb
If I was you, I'd take the job.

Less possible or likely
If + past simple → *would* ('*d*) + verb
If you offered me a discount, I'd buy five.

Talking about something in the past that didn't happen
If + past perfect → *would* + present perfect
If they'd offered me a discount, I would have bought five.

Modals
If you listen to people around you, you can learn a great deal.

Module 11 *Articles*

Use *the* with (1) the names of some countries, (2) superlatives, (3) when there is only one of something and (4) when it has been mentioned before:
The United States is among those countries interested.
China is the biggest producer of these goods.
Who's the supplier in your country?
Leaders of the G8 countries are meeting in Toronto this weekend.
The leaders will hold talks on trade.

Use *a/an* with (1) jobs, (2) singular nouns and (3) some numbers:
I'm a finance director.
This is an international certification mark.
I only have a hundred left.

Use no article (zero article) with (1) cities, towns and most countries and (2) plural nouns:
Madrid is my favourite destination.
When do you fly to China?
Leaders of the G8 countries are meeting in Toronto this weekend.

Module 12 *Indirect questions and tags*

We use indirect questions to make direct questions sound more polite or less direct.

To form the indirect question, move the verb to its position and form in a statement:
Will it attract many people? → *Do you think it will attract many people?*
What do you think is the reason? → *I was wondering what you think the reason is.*
Why did you leave your last job? → *Can you tell me why you left your last job?*

We can use question tags to confirm or check information:
Good marketing is more important than a good product, isn't it?
In the future people will reduce how much they travel by plane, won't they?
You've studied English for three years, haven't you?
You work for Fairtrade, don't you?

MODULE 10

File 10.3 Student C

You are an expert in product placement. During the meeting suggest the following possibilities for developing the band's music and attracting new fans.

- Give out free T-shirts to younger people to wear at fashionable nightclubs.
- Pay Hollywood film makers to let the band appear playing in a new movie.
- On website advertising include a link to a free download of one of the new songs.
- Other?

MODULE 2

File 2.2 Student B

1 headquarters: the head office of a company
2 subsidiary: company owned by a holding company
3 branch: office or group that forms part of a larger company
4 corporation: an organisation formed by a group of companies
5 division: a separate part of a large company

MODULE 3

File 3.2 Student B

You find this correspondence on your desk. Make changes to the schedule in exercise 7 and then confirm details with your partner.

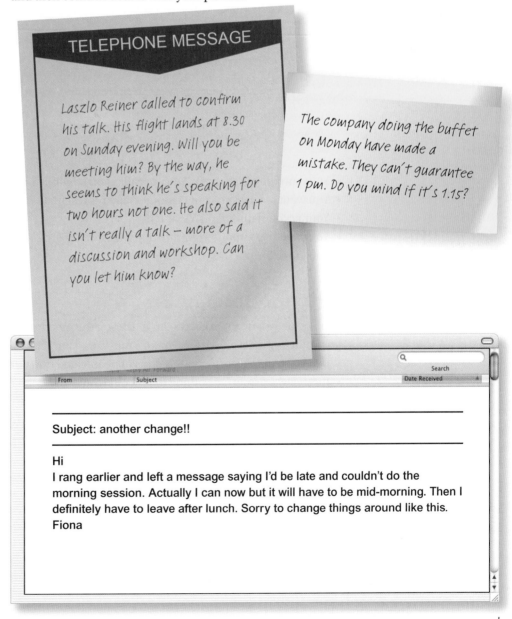

TELEPHONE MESSAGE

Laszlo Reiner called to confirm his talk. His flight lands at 8.30 on Sunday evening. Will you be meeting him? By the way, he seems to think he's speaking for two hours not one. He also said it isn't really a talk – more of a discussion and workshop. Can you let him know?

The company doing the buffet on Monday have made a mistake. They can't guarantee 1 pm. Do you mind if it's 1.15?

Subject: another change!!

Hi
I rang earlier and left a message saying I'd be late and couldn't do the morning session. Actually I can now but it will have to be mid-morning. Then I definitely have to leave after lunch. Sorry to change things around like this.
Fiona

File 3.4 Student B

Your name is Sergiusz Parteka. You telephone Vanessa at Business Circle Conferencing. Postpone your booking for the seminar on online businesses next Tuesday (the 13th) and apologise for the cancellation. Request details of the dates for the next similar seminars after the 13th and find out if the money for the seminar is refunded.

File 9.2 Student B

Call 1

You work in Customer Care at LSA Banking. Take the caller's details and find out what the problem is. You are unable to solve the problem immediately so offer to call back later. Don't forget to take the caller's number.

Call 2

- Your surname is Jakuczik. You are calling on a mobile phone and the battery is low.
- You want to speak to your customer care representative, Mr Vathone.
- Your account number is YE99-087.
- You want to postpone your meeting with him on the 24th in Hong Kong.
- You are in at 7pm (US time).

File 10.2 Student B

You are an expert in market research. During the meeting suggest the following possibilities for developing the band's music and attracting new fans.

- Play different music to focus groups of people and find out what they prefer.
- Interview existing fans online to find out which are their favourite songs from the past and which they don't like any more.
- Find new venues such as smaller fashionable nightclubs for young people.
- Other?

Expressions for the Speaking Test

Answering personal questions

I'm a ... / I come from ... / I live ...
I've lived / worked / studied there for ... / since ...
At the moment, I'm studying / working on ...
I'm interested in ... / I'd like to work in ...

Asking the examiner to repeat a question

Sorry, could you repeat the question, please?
Sorry, can you say that again?

Giving your mini presentation

There are a number of points to consider when ...
First of all, there's ...
Secondly / The second point to remember is ...
For example ...
The final point is ...
It's also important to say ...
In addition to that ... / You also need to consider ...

Discussing

Let's start by ...
What are our options?
One solution would be to ...
How do you feel about that idea?
What do you think? / Do you all agree?

What would happen if we ...?
How about if ...?
The main problem is ...
My other idea is to ...
It'd have the advantage of ...
On the other hand ... / The disadvantage might be ...
One alternative is to ...

I think ... / I agree. / Good idea.
I see your point but ... / Sorry, but ... / I'm not so sure.
I'm sorry but I just can't agree with you there. / I disagree.
Sorry, but I don't quite follow you. / Sorry, I don't understand.
I see what you mean.
That's interesting.
I see. / Really?

Useful writing expressions

Opening salutation

Dear ... / Hi ...

Giving reason for writing

I am writing to ... / in connection with ...
Just a quick note to say ...

Refering to previous contact

With regard to ...
Further to ...
Thanks for your letter / email.
It was good to see you last week ...

Making a suggestion

I would like to suggest ...
How about ...?
What about ...?

Requesting information

Please give me ...
I'd like ...

Thanking

We appreciate ...
We thank you for ...

Apologising

I would like to apologise for ...
We apologise for any inconvenience caused by ...
I'm afraid that ...
I'm sorry about ...

Giving good news

We are delighted to ...
We are pleased to ...
Great news!

Giving bad news

Unfortunately ...
We regret to tell you that ...
The bad news is ...

Explaining reasons

The reason is ...
This is because ...

Requesting

I would be grateful if you could ...
Can you ...?

Offering (help)

Would you like ...?
If you have any further problems, please do not hesitate to contact me.
Do you want me to ...?

Reminding

May I remind you ...
Don't forget ...

Referring to future contact

I / We look forward to ... (-ing)
See you soon.

Closing salutation

Yours faithfully
Yours sincerely
Best regards / wishes
All the best

Announcing

Would all staff note ...
Please note ...

Requesting action

Please ...
I'd be grateful if ...
I'd like to request that ...

Comparing pros and cons

On the one hand ... but on the other ...
One advantage / disadvantage is that ...
One other thing to consider is ...

Balancing and concluding

Despite ... I would still suggest that ...
Overall, I would strongly recommend that ...
The fact that ... makes this ....

Introducing a report

The aim of this report is to ...
This report sets out to ...
The purpose of this report is to ...

Presenting findings

First of all / Secondly ...
It was found that ...
In addition to ...
Alternatively ...
With regard to ...
On the other hand ...

Expressing cause and effect

Because of ...
Due to ...
Further to ...
Following (on from) ...
In order to ...
As a result of ...
... therefore ...

Contrasting

However, ...
Nevertheless ...
Despite ...

Giving additional information

In addition to ...
Furthermore, ...
Moreover, ...

Concluding / Recommending

The findings show that we should ...
In conclusion ...
I would propose / suggest that ...
As a result of ...
This means ...

Module 1

 1.1 **Working from home** (*page 8*)

I = Interviewer   **M** = Michela

I OK, Michela. You work from home now. Can you tell me about a typical day?

M Sure, I always get up around seven and the first thing I do is get the kids ready for school. I take them at eight thirty and then I always start work at nine.

I Do you ever have a day where you decide to have the morning off and start work later?

M No, you can't do that. It's important with home-working to have a timetable and stick to it. If you end up watching TV or doing the cleaning then it isn't for you. So I have lunch at twelve and finish work at two thirty to get the children.

I Was that why you gave up your office job?

M Yes, I wanted to spend more time with the children. It gives me more flexibility. Sometimes I need to work in the evening but usually it isn't a problem.

I So how long have you been doing this kind of work?

M For about five years. I've been with the same company since I left school but with the Internet and technology it's easy now to be at home.

I So your employer doesn't mind.

M No. It means the company saves money on office space and as long as I get the work done, they're happy. Sometimes I still go into work to meet clients and so on. For example, I'm going in nearly every day this week because we have visitors from another company and I can't really invite them over to my house. Besides, it's nice to go in every so often. I like to see people and catch up on the gossip and the news with my colleagues. I miss that side of going into work every day.

I Is there anything else you miss?

M Ermm. No, not really. And I'll tell you what I really don't miss and that's having to spend two hours commuting on the bus and train every day …

 1.2 **Starting a conversation** (*page 11*)

Conversation 1

R = Richard   **W** = Woman   **M** = Marek

R Hello?

W Hello, Richard. I'd like to introduce you to Marek.

R Oh yes. Hello, Marek. How do you do? Nice to meet you at last.

M Hello, Richard. Pleased to meet you too.

W Oh, do you two know each other already?

M Well, we've spoken on the phone a few times.

R But we've never actually met. Anyway, take a seat. Would you both like a coffee?

Conversation 2

A Would you like a coffee?

B Oh thanks.

A Milk?

B Yes, please, and a sugar … thanks.

A So have you enjoyed this morning?

B Yes, it was very interesting. The first speaker was particularly good.

A Is this your first time at one of these events?

B Yes, it is. And you?

A No. I've been coming for years. The company pays and if the location is good then I come. I remember the best year we had was in Monaco …

Conversation 3

M = Marie   **W** = Woman

M May I join you?

W Sure.

M You're a colleague of Martin Obach, aren't you?

W That's right. He works in our Barcelona office. How do you know him?

M We were both at Elcotil together. He left about a year before me.

W Oh, are you Mandy?

M Marie.

W Marie. That's right. Sorry, I knew it began with an M. Yes, Martin said you were doing this course and that I should say hello …

Conversation 4

A Well, this is nice.

B Well, it's quite simple but the food is very traditional and it's popular with the locals. On Sundays I often bring the family here.

A That's nice. How many children do you have?

B Two. Twins. A boy and a girl. They've just started school.

A Wow. Twins.

B And you?

A No, not yet. And have you always lived in Lille?

B Yes, most of my life. I worked in Paris for a while and in your country, of course. But all my relatives are here. What about your family?

A Oh, they're spread out. I see my parents from time to time but my sister lives in Norway with her husband so we don't get together much. Anyway, I know your company is looking for a partner on this Thai project.

B Yes. Is that something you might be interested in …

 1.3 **Exam spotlight** (*page 15*)

E = Examiner   **C** = Candidate

E And where do you live exactly?

C I'm from a small town in northern Switzerland but at the moment I'm studying for a business degree so I live in Zurich.

E What types of business are most successful in your town?

C Err, well, I suppose that tourism is quite important to the area and there are many small farms so agriculture also. Zurich, where I study, is more famous of course for banking and financial services.

E How is working life changing in your country?

C Sorry, can you repeat the question, please?

E Yes, how is working life changing in your country?

C I think that more and more people are moving to the cities or they are commuting in every day. In my opinion, the biggest change has come from technology – but then that's probably true everywhere, not just in my country …

Module 2

2.1 **Benefits and incentives** (*page 16*)

Speaker 1 It's great because usually it means my wife can use the one at home and we even take mine away at weekends. I work for quite a relaxed company and they don't seem to mind how I use it for leisure.

Speaker 2 I thought it wouldn't change the way I worked after the first six months but as they got older it actually became more complicated with getting them to school or if they wanted to do activities in the afternoon. But my boss has been really good about it and some days I can do a half a day if I want and then I might work later on other days – or I take work home, which I don't like doing, but it's the only way …

Speaker 3 It's actually the law now so they had to let me have it. It was only two weeks but at least I had time to help my wife out. Mind you, after all the late nights and crying I was really happy to get back to work for a while and have a rest!

Speaker 4 I've just been promoted from Assistant IT Technician to Chief Operational Network Administrator. It means I get a bit of a pay rise and new business cards with my name on. I'm not sure if I get my own office though.

Speaker 5 The problem for me is that I won't have enough to live on when I'm 60 and I can't afford a private plan. So I'll probably try and keep working for a few more years, and anyway, I heard the government is planning to raise the age of retirement …

2.2 Presentations (page 20)

Extract 1 Good morning and thanks for coming. Today I'd like to tell you about the world's largest document management company. With a turnover of nearly sixteen billion dollars the Xerox Corporation develops and markets innovative technologies with products and solutions that customers depend upon to get the best results for their business. In my brief presentation we'll begin by looking at some of the key figures behind the company's success and how the company is structured. Then I'll give an overview of Xerox around the world and finally I'd like to talk about some of the trends affecting our market and its future growth. If you have any questions, I'll be happy to answer them at the end. So, here you can see, the turnover for last year was nearly sixteen billion dollars, with a final income of 978 million dollars. We operated from our headquarters in Rochester New York State in 160 countries with 55,000 employees, with over half of those in the USA. This next chart shows you how the corporation is split into four divisions. First of all, there's Xerox Global Services …

Extract 2 And finally there's Xerox Innovation with five centres in the United States, Canada and Europe. Note that six percent of revenue was dedicated to research and development last year as the key part of our mission statement is, and I quote, 'to help people find better ways to do great work.' OK, let's move on to look at Xerox around the world in a little more detail. Take a look at this chart, which shows revenue by region. So about half our revenue is from the US market. Then Europe with over five billion dollars and the rest of the world with over two. One thing I'd like to point out is …

Extract 3 Finally, how is the market for the document industry looking? Well, it would be unrecognisable to the people who founded the original company in 1906 and even compared to the second half of the twentieth century. More and more offices are moving from black and white printing to colour and from paper documents to electronic documents. These are clearly the future opportunities and areas of growth in what is a total market worth an estimated 112 billion dollars …

So that brings me to the end of my presentation. Thanks for listening. I hope it's been of interest. Are there any questions?

2.3 Pausing (page 21)

Presenter Good morning / and thanks for coming. / Today / I'd like to tell you about / the world's / largest / document / management / company. / With a turnover of nearly sixteen billion dollars / the Xerox Corporation develops / and markets / innovative technologies / with products and solutions / that customers depend upon to get the best results / for their business. / In my brief presentation / we'll begin by looking at / some of the key figures / behind the company's success / and how the company is structured. / Then / I'll give an overview of Xerox around the world / and finally / I'd like to talk about some of the trends / affecting our

market / and its future growth. / If you have any questions, / I'll be happy to answer them at the end. /

2.4 Intonation and stress (page 21)

Presenter Good morning / and thanks for coming. / Today / I'd like to tell you about / the world's / largest / document / management / company. / With a turnover of nearly sixteen billion dollars / the Xerox Corporation develops / and markets / innovative technologies / with products and solutions / that customers depend upon to get the best results / for their business. / In my brief presentation / we'll begin by looking at / some of the key figures / behind the company's success / and how the company is structured. / Then / I'll give an overview of Xerox around the world / and finally / I'd like to talk about some of the trends / affecting our market / and its future growth. / If you have any questions, / I'll be happy to answer them at the end. /

Module 3

3.1 Advice on franchises (page 27)

T = Trainer   **M** = Man

T So. That's the end of my talk. Are there any questions? Yes?

M Thanks for your talk. It was very interesting. I've been thinking of starting my own business and I wondered what you thought of franchises.

T That's a good question. In general it's important when you are thinking of becoming a franchisee to be someone who likes to follow rules and have support from others. Entrepreneurs tend to be people who don't like following tried and tested routes, so if you don't like doing what other people want, then franchising isn't for you.

Secondly, I'd say make sure that the brand is strong and that it's something you are interested in. For example, making and selling pizzas might be profitable but do you want to be doing it for the next five years? I also think you need to like hard work. People shouldn't think that running a franchise is less work than being a sole trader.

Finally, there's the money. You still need start-up capital. This can be as low as five thousand pounds and as high as two hundred and thirty thousand pounds for a well-known brand like Domino's Pizza …

3.2 Planning a seminar (1) (page 28)

Recorded message Thank you for calling Business Circle Conferencing. Please state your name and address. Then give the name of the event you'd like information on and we will send it to you immediately. Please speak after the tone.

Ray Hello. This is Mr Ray Naunton. That's N-A-U-N-T-O-N. I'm coming to the event next week called 'Launching your business online' and so you've already got my details. Anyway, the reason I'm calling is that I won't be able to arrive in time for registration and the buffet on the Sunday evening. My train doesn't arrive until nine fifteen, so I'm going to take a taxi straight to the hotel. So I probably won't get to the training centre until Monday morning. I hope that's OK. Anyway it's just to confirm that I will be there for the course. Oh, and could someone send me the schedule for the two days? You can email it to me at r dot naunton at worldsyouroyster dot com. Worldsyouroyster is all one word. That's w-o-r-l-d-s-y-o-u-r-o-y-s-t-e-r. And all in lower case. Thank you.

3.3 Planning a seminar (2) (page 28)

Kirsten Hello, Kirsten speaking.

Vanessa Hi, Kirsten. It's Vanessa. I'm just calling to check details for the group on Sunday evening.

Kirsten Sure. Security are opening the room at three. Is that early enough?

Vanessa Yes, the buffet won't be setting up until four thirty so that's plenty of time. I'll get there at four and I don't think anyone will be arriving before five. According to my records, we have twelve. Is that right?

Kirsten Yes. Everyone has confirmed. Oh, that reminds me. We've had a message from Mr Naunton to say he won't be here until after nine so he's checking straight into the hotel. There's no point in inviting him to come after then, is there? I mean, I assume that we'll have finished by nine.

Vanessa By seven, I hope. Well, I hope they'll have gone by then! If they want to get to know each other any longer, they can use the hotel bar.

Kirsten Fine. I think that's everything, then. Do you need me to be there?

Vanessa No. There's no point in both of us interrupting our weekend. It doesn't need two of us.

Kirsten Great. See you on Monday. Bye.

Vanessa Bye.

 3.4 Leaving messages (*page 30*)

Call 1 Hi, Vanessa. It's Ralph again. Sorry, I forgot to ask earlier if you can send me details of next month's seminars. I've got two people who really need some help with spreadsheets and accounting software. I remember you said that you had some computer courses planned. Anyway, send me details on those and anything else you have coming up. Thanks. Oh. You can email it to me if that's easier. It's R for Ralph. Dot. Hensher. At Henckel. That's H-E-N-C-K-E-L dot D-E. Thanks. Bye.

Call 2 Hello. My name is Maria Monblot. The reason I'm calling is that I have a booking for next week's business breakfast meeting. I'm afraid I won't be able to attend but I would like to come to next month's instead. I assume it is on the last Wednesday of the month as usual. Please confirm this. You've already got my number but just in case, it's 768 4556.

Call 3 Hello. This is Jochen Anderson. I am booked in to run the seminar on design on the 25th. I've just received the schedule for the day and it appears that I am speaking at nine thirty. That isn't what I agreed with you. We said I would be at eleven and that I would have ninety minutes, not one hour. You've also described it as a talk but I'm giving a workshop. Please get back to me about this as soon as possible. I'll be in my office between two and five o'clock.

Call 4 Hi, Vanessa. It's Kirsten. Just to let you know that Jochen Anderson is trying to get hold of you. He left a message on my home number to say he isn't happy about the schedule for the 25th. I haven't got the details with me so I can't help really. I'm sorry, but can you call him back? He only needs the time changing and something about the title. I'm sure one of the other speakers won't mind changing. You know what he's like. See you tomorrow.

Call 5 Hello. This is Bryan in security. I'm returning your call about having the building open on Sunday. I'm just calling to say that's fine. I'll be here at midday anyway so it'll be OK for three o'clock. If there's anything else you can call me any time on my mobile. It's 07786 678 8890.

 3.5 Taking notes and messages (*page 33*)

Vanessa Hello, Business Circle Conferencing.

Jochen Hello. Can I speak to Kirsten, please?

Vanessa I'm sorry, she's not here today. My name's Vanessa. Can I help you?

Jochen This is Jochen Anderson.

Vanessa Oh, hello, Mr Anderson. Kirsten said you phoned and I tried calling you at your office.

Jochen Well, I'm on my mobile. Anyway, it's about the schedule for the training event. It isn't what we agreed.

Vanessa Sorry, let me check. So that's the event on the 25th.

Jochen That's right. And it says I'm speaking at nine thirty.

Vanessa And you're supposed to be speaking at eleven. Yes, well I'm sure we can change it.

Jochen Yes, but actually I think the afternoon would be better. After lunch. Can I speak at two pm? Then I can arrive in the morning.

Vanessa I see. So that's two in the afternoon. I'll have to check with another presenter and then call you back. Could you give me your mobile number?

Jochen Certainly. It's 0778 890 8895.

Vanessa Let me read that back to you. 0778 890 8895.

Jochen That's right.

Vanessa I'll call you back in about an hour.

Jochen Good. Thank you.

 3.6 Exam spotlight (*page 34*)

N = Narrator   **M** = Man   **W** = Woman

N Part One. Questions 1–12.

You will hear three telephone conversations or messages. Write one or two words or a number in the numbered spaces on the notes or forms below. You will hear each recording twice.

Conversation One. Questions 1–4.

Look at the form below. You will hear a woman telephoning about a problem with her subscription to a business magazine. You have fifteen seconds to read through the form. Now listen, and fill in the spaces.

M Thank you for calling Business Monthly. Please state your name, the name of your company or organisation and your address. If you already have a subscription with us please give your subscription number and the reason for your call.

W Hello. This is Cynthia Perkins – that's P-E-R-K-I-N-S. I'm the research manager at RAVE solutions. That's R-A-V-E solutions. You've got our address on record. I'm calling about our current subscription. The number is IL0378JUL. We paid for twelve issues but we've only received eleven. Please send the June edition of the magazine. Thank you very much.

N Now listen to the recording again.

 3.7 Exam spotlight (*page 35*)

N = Narrator   **T** = Tom   **M** = Mari

N Conversation Two. Questions 5–8.

Look at the form below. You will hear a man telephoning a production company about a training video. You have fifteen seconds to read through the form. Now listen, and fill in the spaces.

T Hello, this is Tom Yishan from Bright Star publishing. Could I speak to Mari Jones-Lumley, please?

M Speaking. Hello, Tom. How are you?

T Fine, thanks. Look, Mari, it's about this training video you're making for us.

M Oh no, what's happened?

T No, don't worry. Everything's fine. It's just that you know you wanted to film in the printing factory, if you could. Well, I spoke to the manager and that's OK with them except that the dates we agreed aren't convenient for them. They want to know if you can put it back by ten days.

M I'd normally say yes, Tom, but we've already postponed this twice. I can't go on telling my team to cancel. Anyway, I think we have another project then.

T I'm really sorry, Mari, but it's out of my control.

M OK. Can you check with the printing manager if two weeks later would be OK and I'll have to check with my people.

T Two weeks? So that's the 25th?

M Right.

T No problem. I'll try and call him now and get back to you to confirm.

N Now listen to the recording again.

 3.8 Exam spotlight (*page 35*)

N = Narrator   **P** = Personnel Assistant   **R** = Rachel

N Conversation Three. Questions 9–12.

Look at the form below. You will hear a woman telephoning another department in her company about a job applicant. You have fifteen seconds to read through the message pad. Now listen, and fill in the spaces.

P Hello. Personnel.

R Hello, this is Rachel in IT. It's about the application of that new graduate which Michael sent over. Can I have a word with him?

P Sorry Rachel, he won't be in till tomorrow, but you can leave him a message.

R Thanks. I'm afraid I've got a problem with the application form. Rufus has done his diploma in IT at the local college but he hasn't filled in the section on references. I really need to speak to his tutor. Can Michael get hold of the contact details for him – his telephone number or email will do.

P OK. Is that all then?

R Err, I also need to know when Michael has scheduled him for interview. I think it might be tomorrow but I'm not sure. If it is tomorrow, has somebody confirmed that with Rufus because when I spoke to him briefly yesterday, he didn't seem to know anything about it.

P Oh dear. Well, I'll give Michael your message and let you know.

R Well, I'll be in a meeting for the rest of the day so leave me a message about tomorrow, and someone had better ring Rufus and tell him he has an interview. And let me know how long he thinks it will take. I'm pretty busy.

P Right. Will do.

N Now listen to the recording again.

Module 4

 4.1   Advertising on the web (*page 37*)

Speaker Imagine you have a new product or a new service and you want the world to know about it. One way would be to write the advertisement onto ten or a hundred or a thousand pieces of paper and drop them from the sky over your town or city. Someone on the ground might pick one up and read it. Maybe two or three people. On the other hand the wind might blow them away.

Now imagine doing the same thing but this time throwing them into the air with adverts for every other product or service in the world. You probably wouldn't do it, would you? Well, unfortunately, that's what it's like to advertise on the Internet.

Trying to make your product, service or website known to the rest of the Internet community can be very, very frustrating. Not only making it known, but getting visitors to actually visit the site can seem impossible. But there are ways to overcome the impossible when advertising on the Internet, as long as you follow three rules.

So, rule number one. The first thing is to remember that people use search engines. So whenever someone types in a keyword linked to your business, your site needs to appear in the top 50 or so listings in all of the major search engines. Any lower and no one will ever find you.

My second rule is that it's a good idea to spend some useful time and effort on getting your links on other sites. This is an excellent, though very time-consuming way to increase visitors. You can do this by sharing links with other companies, so they have a link on your site and you put one on theirs. Or perhaps through a site review which recommends your products. Also remember that the more links you have elsewhere, the more likely people are to find you through a search engine.

My third tip is never to pay for advertising on the web. I think that unless you have a very good reason, it's a waste of money. With so many ways to get free advertising, I've found very little reason to pay for things like banners to promote my site.

So those are my three starting points for anyone thinking of web advertising. Before we finish don't forget that a memorable domain name that people can easily type will help. Email campaigns can work and are an easy way to get traffic to the site, though it doesn't last long. What might be better is to have a monthly newsletter, which people sign up for. I've found this to be very effective and more positive than sending spam. Then there are contests with prizes or anything free – maybe some software or cool graphics.

Once you've got people visiting the site, keep statistics on how many people visit per day and how often people return to the site. In other words, find out who they are. How old they are. Where they come from. What they like doing in their free time. You can get this kind of information by asking them to subscribe to your newsletter, for example …

 4.2   A bad delegator (*page 41*)

Manager Hi, Harry. Sorry to bother you but I'm so busy. Could you help me? I know you're busy too but I have a meeting with the managing director tomorrow and I don't have time to do the schedules for next week. I know you did them last time I was off sick so I thought you could do them again. I don't want to give you anything too difficult, do I? So if I give you this … Sorry, I haven't had time to sort through it but you'll work it out. OK, great. Sorry, must go. If you have any questions … err, ask Mary. I think she did the schedules last time I was on holiday so she can help too. Fine. Bye!

 4.3   Sentence stress (*page 41*)

Can I borrow your **expertise** in something?

I've asked **you** because …

Let me know how it's going **once** a week, please.

I'll need a report on this with your findings **and** your recommendations.

So, let's go through this **one** more time to check it's clear.

One thing you **might** want to think about is …

You've done a **great** job on this!

I've got a job here that will **really** interest you …

I'd like you to be in charge of **all** of it.

What are you going to **do**?

Feel free to call me if you have **any** questions.

Can you give this priority because they need it as **soon** as possible?

The deadline for this is **next** Thursday.

Module 5

 5.1   An interview with an art consultant (1) (*page 47*)

I = Interviewer   **AC** = Art consultant

I I'd like to begin by asking you to imagine that I've been asked to find some art for my company's offices. Where would I start?

AC Well, the first stage in selecting art is normally for one of our art consultants to visit you on site to assess the location, the size of the area and the style of the building, and so on.

I How much difference does it make where I actually put the paintings?

AC A great deal. Art needs to be placed taking into account the function of a space. Different types of art are appropriate for different areas. Once we have an idea about what kind of work it is you do and how the space is used, then we begin to find artworks and present a selection of art for your business and building. We can do this on-site or you can visit our galleries. The whole thing is a two-way collaborative process.

I So you already have the painting?

AC Yes, or we can ask an artist to create works for your specific space. In this case, the client has some input but it's important to remember when choosing workplace art that art is not your brand. If you ask the artist to emphasise your company image in some way, you'll just end up with bad art. Either way, you have an art consultant who oversees and project manages the production of any commissioned artwork, and makes sure it's completed and installed on time and within budget. And that also includes fitting appropriate lighting and any other maintenance and fitting …

5.2 An interview with an art consultant (2) (page 47)

I = Interviewer   AC = Art consultant

I One thing I don't understand is how a company ever decides what to choose. I mean, art is such a personal thing. How does anyone ever agree?

AC Well, that's true. I think it's important that you don't set up committees or anything. If you have a workforce of 300 and you ask everyone, you'll get 300 different answers. No, you need to keep it small. Just one or two people. But choosing art for your offices isn't necessarily about choosing what the individual likes. The real benefits for a business are that the artwork gives a positive image to clients.

I So what's a typical type of art?

AC It's so varied but in general I suggest something strong and bold. If it's just light colours that no one can really see, it's pointless. You need art which shows your clients you have good taste and that you are successful.

I I often go into buildings and look at modern art and think, 'What is that? It isn't of anything. No people. Nothing.' Why do so many companies choose it?

AC There are a number of reasons, other than the fact that the managing director might like it. You don't want art that will offend anyone. So a painting of a man and a woman with no clothes on is a bad idea. Similarly, a landscape or a painting of the countryside is the sort of thing you have in your living room at home and doesn't look very corporate. Also the art needs to say what kind of company you are. Most companies want to give clients the message that says we're modern and we're planning for the future. A classical painting says we're old and traditional. A painting by a young, modern painter gives a more positive image. And remember, it doesn't have to be a painting. A sculpture in the reception area can be very effective, for example.

I Finally, all this must be very expensive. How does a company justify thousands of pounds on this kind of thing?

AC It can be expensive but of course many people rent works from us – for as little as ten pounds a week. It also means that if you change your mind after a year or so, it's easy to change the piece.

I That sounds like a good idea …

5.3 Some opinions on art (page 49)

Speaker 1 But what is it? Is that a head? Or is it an animal? I can't see how that is art. I mean, it doesn't look like anything real.

Speaker 2 I agree with you that this is nice. It reminds me of being in a café in somewhere like Paris but if you put it here no one will see it. It isn't bold enough for this area. No, we need something else.

Speaker 3 This is beautiful but perhaps it would look better in someone's office. It's the sort of painting to help you relax.

Speaker 4 Well, I'm not really the right person to ask. I never go to art galleries but this looks like what you see in cathedrals. It doesn't tell you what our company is about. When people come into reception, they'll think it's a Roman temple, not a hi-tech business. Let's have something up-to-date.

Speaker 5 This is quite good for reception because it shows a man thinking, which is quite a good image for our company. It says to the visitor that this is a company with ideas. That we're constantly considering the future …

5.4 Report on a meeting (page 53)

RS = Robert Samuelson   HS = Hugo Sata   DZ = Dahlia Zille

RS OK. Point one is about the conference. It starts on the 8th but I think someone should go out early on the 6th. What do you think, Hugo?

HS Sorry, but I did that last year and sat around for a day. There was really nothing to do. I think if we go early it shouldn't be until the 7th. It really isn't worth it.

RS OK, that's fine. Do you agree, Dahlia?

DZ Sure. Do you want me to go?

RS Is that OK with you, Hugo?

HS Absolutely.

RS OK, point two. I'm assuming you're dealing with that, Dahlia.

DZ Yes, I've already found a good hotel near the fair and I'll book the flights.

RS Great. Now what about this idea to sponsor a reception for delegates? In the past other publishers have sponsored drinks and buffets in the evening. I'd like some views on this. Hugo?

HS Well, they certainly attract people looking for a free dinner! I wonder if the evening's a good idea though.

RS Sorry, Hugo, I don't understand.

HS Well, maybe if we just offer drinks at the stand at lunchtime, we'll get more people actually looking at books and talking to us.

DZ That's a good idea, Hugo.

RS Yes, nice idea. Can you organise that, Hugo?

HS What's my budget?

RS Erm. Let me check with accounts after the meeting and I'll tell you.

DZ Sorry, Robert, but before we finish there's a problem with the prices in the brochures.

RS Really?

DZ Yes, the brochures have been updated with our list for next year but the prices are the same. We can get them reprinted but not in time for Seattle.

RS Oh no. You're joking!

DZ Sorry …

RS Any ideas?

HS Let's just include the price list as separate from the brochure. We can say these are new for next year.

DZ But won't it show that prices have gone up? People will be able to compare next year's with this year's.

HS True. What do you think, Robert?

RS Well, we could include some offers on the new price list and show some prices haven't gone up.

DZ That might work.

HS I don't think we have a choice, Robert!

RS OK. I'll prepare that. Right, Hugo, Dahlia? Anything else?

 5.5 Exam spotlight (1) *(page 54)*

E = Examiner   **P** = Pierre   **Er** = Erica

E I'm going to give each of you a choice of three topics. I'd like you to choose one of the topics and give a short presentation on it for about a minute. You will have about a minute to prepare for this and you can make notes if you wish while you prepare. After you have finished your talk, your partner will ask you a question. All right? Here are your topics. Choose one of the topics to talk about. You can make notes.

 5.6 Exam spotlight (2) *(page 54)*

E All right. Now Pierre, which topic have you chosen, A, B or C?

P Topic A.

E OK. Would you like to talk about what you think is important when placing a newspaper advert?

P OK. So there are a number of points to consider when placing a newspaper advert because you want it to be as effective as possible. First of all, there's the reader to consider. You need to know who you are trying to reach. So, for example, if your product is for teenagers, you need to put your advert into the type of newspapers or magazines they'll read. Right, the second point to remember is that once you've chosen the best newspaper, you also need to consider where it will appear. Obviously, the front page is good but it's the most expensive place. That's also true for the back page. So look at the paper and decide which parts are most interesting to readers. Maybe it's the sports pages or perhaps it will be in the TV section. Again, this will help you reach the right kind of reader. Something else is the appearance of the advertisement. You need something to get the reader's attention like bright colours, perhaps a photograph or some of the words need to be very large. I think that all helps ...

E Thank you. Now, Erica, can you ask Pierre your question about his talk?

Er Yes, people say that newspaper advertising isn't as effective as, say, a TV commercial. Do you agree with this?

P Well, I think that it's true that TV commercials are sometimes very effective but newspaper advertising can also be ...

Module 6

 6.1 Employment case studies *(page 57)*

S = Speaker

Speaker 1 I'd really had enough. The people there were great and I really liked my supervisor but it was just too boring. I only started in order to make a bit of extra money when I was a student. I didn't intend to stay this long and especially not after I finished my degree. So they said they were sad to see me go but they understood. Anyway, I told them when I wanted to leave, but they said I didn't need to worry about what it said in my contract, so I didn't actually have to work the full four weeks ...

Speaker 2 Someone had to go. We haven't been getting the orders for a while so it was clear that they'd be laying people off sooner or later. Anyway, I thought rather than wait I'd go now and take the money. It was a good deal and it gives me a few months to find another job.

Speaker 3 Well, it's a good position and suits anyone who doesn't want to work every day of the week. We had three applicants but it was obvious who was right. I think Samantha will be perfect. She's keen and flexible which works well for both sides. And I think she can work at weekends, too, so that'll come in useful. Especially around Christmas time ...

Speaker 4 I couldn't believe it. OK, so I've been late a couple of times but my boss said it wasn't a problem as long as I made up the extra hours in the evening. And then someone, and I can guess who, reported me. You know, that one who works in accounts who's always gossiping about other people. She said I'd been taking stationery from the cupboard and using it for personal correspondence. The manager asked me to come into the office so I could see what was coming. I wasn't going to wait around and get a lecture. I was through that door before anyone could stop me.

Speaker 5 The first thing I'm going to do is take the family on a nice long holiday while we can still afford it. Then I'll start thinking about what I'll do next when I get home. There's plenty of time, though for someone of my age I'm not sure what I'll get. Maybe I'll just work part-time until my pension begins. It's only seven years. Pity really. I would have liked to have stayed on 'til retirement. Mind you, it's worse for some of the others. They've got another twenty years to go. I mean, where will they get another job round here ...

Module 7

 7.1 Selling *(page 71)*

C = Customer   **S** = Salesperson

Salesperson 1

C Well, June is always a little difficult because demand falls and we have to wait until July again before things pick up.

S So is extra advertising something you might be interested in?

C Maybe, though we have tried that before. You know, in local magazines and so on.

S Perhaps radio or a mailshot could be useful?

C Local radio's an interesting idea. I haven't thought about it, really.

Salesperson 2

This is our latest XR5. It's a huge improvement on the previous 2007 model because they've updated it with a number of key features such as backseat airbags for the kids, half a cubic metre extra in the back for luggage, and the braking system is state-of-the-art. It'll do zero to 70 in five seconds and of course there's air conditioning. The dashboard is particularly interesting because it will tell you when the tyres need more air pressure or if it's due a service check-up ...

Salesperson 3

C Hello.

S Hello, Ray. It's Ivan from Beavis Supplies.

C Oh hi, Ivan. How are you? It's been a long time.

S Yes, I'm afraid I've been off sick for a couple of weeks.

C Oh, I'm sorry to hear that.

S Well, I'm OK now. How are things with you?

C Pretty good. We're busy.

S That's good. So is there anything I can help you with at the moment?

C As a matter of fact, I need some letterheads fairly soon.

S So shall I put you down for your usual order?

C Actually, I was thinking we could do something with the design.

S Sure, what did you have in mind exactly?

Salesperson 4

S Erm, well yes, err this is quite good. It has a diary section here, you know from January to February. And, err, I think at the back there's an address book ... oh, I thought there was. Maybe there used to be. Anyway ...

C Is this cover leather?

S Erm, yes. Well, yes, it feels like leather. I know we can get them in black and red as well as brown. I know it's proved much more popular than the old plastic sort.

C And how much does it cost to put our logo on the front?

S Logo? Sure. Right. Yes, that would look good, wouldn't it. Well, let me ring the office and maybe they can give me, I mean give you a price on that … one moment …

Salesperson 5

C1 Hello?

S Hello, is that Mr Hawkes?

C1 Yes, who's this?

S Hello, Mr Hawkes, this is Martin calling from Warm and Cosy. Mr Hawkes, I was wondering if you'd mind answering a few questions about your home this evening.

C1 Why?

S Well, it happens that a representative from Warm and Cosy will be in your area tomorrow and he'll be available to advise you on any home improvements you might be thinking of …

C2 Hello?

S Hello, is that Mrs Jones?

C2 Yes, speaking.

S Hello, Mrs Jones, this is Martin calling from Warm and Cosy and I was wondering …

Module 8

 8.1 Assessing training needs *(page 77)*

M = Manager   **S** = Sergio

M Come in … oh hello, Sergio.

S Hi. Sorry for being late. Someone needed to speak to me. Anyway, I've looked at those courses you suggested doing …

M And?

S Yes, they both look good. I'm interested in doing both of them.

M Good. I thought they might help with your new role.

S Yes, well. It involves telling people what to do but I'm also working with other managers too.

M OK. So would you like to enrol for both of them?

S Yes, but I can't afford to take any more time off this month. I'm already behind.

M But these are online. You don't need to go away.

S What do you mean?

M Online means you train by using the Internet. I think you receive articles to read and you have a tutor who contacts you by email.

S Oh, I see. I remember doing something similar by post. I got books to read and had some exercises.

M Yes, like that but on the Internet. It's great because you don't have to go away and you arrange things around your work.

S The problem is that I'd prefer to have a course with other people in a room. You get lots of new ideas that way. Especially on a course called Team Building. If I do it online, I won't have the opportunity for networking with people. And you can ask the tutor questions.

M You're right, but I also think many online courses even have a place where you communicate with other people on the course.

S Hmm. But I don't think it is the same. Besides, if I'm working at my desk I always stop to answer the phone or someone asks me to do something.

M Well, why not do it from home?

S I don't understand …

M Take an afternoon off and use your computer from home. That way no one can interrupt you. The other thing is that if you want to do both courses, it's cheaper if you do them online …

 8.2 Good and bad listeners *(page 81)*

Conversation 1

A So what happened?

B Well, we all went out. We had the restaurant booked for eight. Anyway, everyone seemed to be having a good time, but it all went wrong in the end.

A Really?

B We had dinner and then of course they wanted to discuss the final part of the deal. I'd wanted to leave it until the morning but they were keen to finish things off.

A I see. Why do you think that is?

B I guess they were under pressure from their bosses to get a deal and go home …

Conversation 2

A Hello, Grainger and Co.

B Hello, I have a problem with a coffee maker that you produce. Can I speak to …

A Sorry, let me just stop you there. Can I have your name first, please?

B It's Dana Lund.

A Well, what you need to do, Mr Lund, is to take it back to the place of purchase first. We only deal with online purchases …

B But I bought it from your website!

Conversation 3

A … so I'm not really sure how I'm going to handle this one. I don't think they really believe I know how to run a project.

B Well, of course the answer is simple, isn't it? You just have to let them know that you're the boss. They're paid to listen to you. If they don't like it, they can leave.

A I know, but I want to work in a good atmosphere where people feel motivated …

B I know you do, but can I tell you what I think? I think …

Conversation 4

A OK. So that brings me to the end. Are there any questions?

B Sorry. Let me check I've understood you.

A Sure. Go ahead.

B So what you're saying is that we can virtually halve our costs if we restructure in this way. Is that right?

A That's right. It won't be pleasant. It will mean job losses but I don't think we have a choice.

B Yes. I see what you mean.

A Of course, if anyone has any other ways of approaching this, then let's hear them …

 8.3 Responding to a letter of complaint *(page 83)*

Le Fevre Hello, Fred. It's Jean here.

Perrot Hi, Jean.

Le Fevre Sorry to bother you but I've just received a letter from a client here. She isn't happy and I need to reply as soon as possible.

Perrot Really? What's the problem?

Le Fevre Well, she's referring to a computer course in PowerPoint on the 25th April. Two people from her company Hollers and Fry were on the course.

Perrot I think you mean on the 26th actually. The 25th was a Sunday.

Le Fevre Oh, OK. Anyway, you know about it?

Perrot Well, I wasn't here. I was supposed to be but I had to take the day off work because one of my children – she was sick. My wife was away so as a result I rang in early to see if we could get a replacement trainer. Anyway, we did and he was a little late. However, he's good. I know his work. And we added the lost time on to the end of each of the two days. Is that what they're complaining about?

Le Fevre Well, that's one thing. I didn't know you added the time back on. That's useful to know. And it's also because of a room change or something.

Perrot OK. Well, that's because of them sending two people. Despite having told them the course was full and we could only take one of their people they still sent two. So rather than send one of them home we were able to switch training rooms and deal with it.

Le Fevre So that sounds like their fault. OK. And this last thing I'm less concerned about.

Perrot What's that?

Le Fevre Oh, she says 'my staff inform me that the approach of the trainer was to let participants "discover" solutions to problems rather than being told what to do'.

Perrot I'm sorry, Jean, but I'm always telling our computer trainers to follow a discovery approach. To do less talking and let trainees find out for themselves. And anyway, everyone else always gives us positive feedback because of this approach.

Le Fevre I know. I understand. Don't worry. That's all I need to know. I'm sure I can sort it out. Thanks, Fred.

Perrot Bye.

 8.4 Exam spotlight *(page 85)*

N = Narrator   S = Speaker

N Section 1. Questions 1–5. You will hear five people talking about training courses. For each recording, decide which course the person is referring to. Write one letter (A–H) next to the number of the recording. Do not use any letter more than once. After you have listened once, replay each recording. You have fifteen seconds to read the list A–H.

Now listen, and decide which course each speaker is referring to.

N One

S1 Actually, it didn't tell me more than I already do. I suppose the parts on how to answer questions and working on convincing people was OK. But how to stand and when to use your hands seemed a bit excessive. And when he talked about visual aids I wondered if everyone else thought it was as pointless as me.

N Two

S2 We tend to cover areas such as planning and organisation. Then I give exercises on how to simplify your language, because so many of us seem to think that on paper we need to be more formal than when we speak. The trouble with that is that I find many people make quite simple information quite complicated.

N Three

S3 I really found the group activities useful. You know, we played some games and did roleplays to see what it was like to work with others and how to facilitate groups of people so they pull on each other's strengths and weaknesses.

N Four

S4 I've just started in HR so it'll be helpful in the future when departments contact me about finding people to join them. It's amazing how much you can tell about someone by the way they sit or their body language as well as asking the right questions. I also learnt about different methods of testing to assess characters and potential.

N Five

S5 You often think that people don't understand or wonder why teams don't get on. So it was interesting to think about how we all view the world in different ways. Even down to how we say hello and shake hands or bow. For example, did you know that it's rude to talk about business straight away in Brazil?

N Now listen to the recording again.

 8.5 Exam spotlight *(page 85)*

N = Narrator   S = Speaker

N Section 2. Questions 6–10. You will hear another five short recordings. Each person is speaking on the phone. For each recording, decide the main reason for the call. Write one letter (A–H) next to the number of the recording. Do not use any letter more than once. After you have listened once, replay each

recording. You have fifteen seconds to read the list of reasons A–H.

Now listen, and decide the reason for each speaker's call.

N Six

S1 Hi Joe. I'm just phoning to say I'll be in at three o'clock as planned. They had said there would be problems on the planes because of a strike but it seems to be OK now so I'll see you tomorrow.

N Seven

S2 Hi. It's me. It's about the meeting you couldn't come to. Sorry your train was delayed, by the way. Anyway, just to say it was agreed we should start work on the 25th and Hamid thinks we'll make the schedule we talked about if we bring in one more person to act as site manager. I said I thought this would be OK as the budget allowed for it.

N Eight

S3 Good morning. I'm calling about your advert for a secretary that was in today's newspaper. I applied for that post two weeks ago and heard nothing back from you. I really think that if you didn't like my application, you should have at least replied and let me know. Instead I discovered it in the paper!

N Nine

S4 I was wondering if you could call Lucy for me. I think I left the plans for the Royale Project at her office. If you have time, could you go round and pick them up because I'll need them for tomorrow. Sorry to bother you with it but I'm in our other office all day. I've been trying to call her all morning but she must be out. Can you try her this afternoon?

N Ten

S5 Hello, I'm calling about the overdraft facility you offer to customers with online banking. I was wondering how I can get it. Also, I'm not sure how to get an online account, so maybe you can tell me what I need to do.

N Now listen to the recording again.

Module 9

 9.1 Automated voicemail systems (1) *(page 90)*

C = Caller   M = Machine

C Hello, I'd like to speak to …

M Hello. Thank you for calling GH Loans Customer Care. You will now hear a number of options. Please press the option you require. For a statement, press 1, for early repayment, press 2, for any other enquiry or to speak to one of our operators, press 3 … Thank you.

C Hello, I'm calling about …

M Thank you for calling GH Loans. Please note that your call may be monitored for quality assurance and training purposes.

M We're sorry but all of our operators are currently unavailable to take your call. Please hold. Your call is important to us.

M Hello. You're through to our loans department.

C Could you put me through to someone …

M To help us deal with your call quickly and efficiently, please answer the following questions with 'yes' or 'no'. Do you currently have an account with …

9.2 Automated voicemail systems (2) *(page 90)*

O = Operator   C = Caller

O Hello, you're through to Katrina. How can I help you this morning?

C Oh hello, it's with regard to a statement I received. I think there's been a mistake.

O OK. One moment, please. Can I take your name, please?

C Yes, it's Abi Kaye.

O Can you spell that for me?

C Sure. Abi. A-B-I. Kaye. K-A-Y-E.

O And do you have an account number?

C Yes. TI3662.

O Sorry. Was that T for Thailand, I as in India?

C That's correct.

O And for security can I have your date of birth?

C The 21st April 1981.

O That's fine, Ms Kaye. So how can I help you?

C Well, I paid off part of my loan early last month but I received a statement from you this morning and it isn't on the statement. Could you tell me if the payment has gone through?

O Right. I don't see it. Can you bear with me for a second? I'm just going to put you on hold.

C Sure.

O Hello. Sorry to keep you waiting. I'm afraid I can't find a record of it. How much was it for?

C Five thousand euros.

O I'll have to check this for you. Can I call you back?

C Yes, please.

O What's your number, Ms Kaye?

C Zero one seven, two double four, three nine two nine.

O So that was zero one seven, two double four, three nine two nine.

C That's right. What time do you think you'll call back because I have to go out now?

O When would suit you?

C At four?

O That's fine. Speak to you then. Goodbye.

C Bye.

Module 10

 10.1 Problems and solutions (1) *(page 100)*

Linda Hi, Roger. It's Linda. Sorry, it's really noisy here. I hope you can hear this. I'm at the site. It's going well but we have a problem. The windows have just arrived for the south side of the building. They'd be fine if it wasn't for the fact that four of them don't fit. They seem to be about one point five centimetres too wide for the spaces. I think it's a manufacturing fault but if I send them straight back, the manufacturer'll probably say it's the architect's fault. What do you think I should do? Can you call me back as soon as you get this? We can't afford any more mistakes. I don't know, Roger. If I'd known this project was going to cause this much trouble, I would have said forget it! Anyway, call me back on my mobile if you get this message.

 10.2 Problems and solutions (2) *(page 100)*

Linda Linda speaking.

Roger Hi, Linda. It's me, Roger. Thanks for your message. I would have rung you straight back if I'd managed to get hold of the architect. He's in Madrid or something.

Linda So did you speak to the window people?

Roger Yes, and as you predicted they said if they'd received the right specifications from the plans in the first place, there wouldn't have been a problem.

Linda Well, I bet when you get the architect, he'll say it's their fault.

Roger Anyway, we can worry about whose fault it is later. The main thing is to find a solution. And quickly. What are our options?

Linda Well, if we send the windows back to the manufacturer, it'll take about sixteen weeks to have them redone. That'll include the architect doing new designs.

Roger Sixteen weeks is ages. We'll go way behind schedule. The client would never agree.

Linda Yes, I know, so my other idea is to make the space for the windows wider by cutting into the area around the window. If we

did this, it'd have the advantage of using our people already on site so I wouldn't be paying them for doing nothing. It's a bit expensive but I think it'd take about two weeks.

Roger Good idea. And what you save in time means it'll be cheaper overall. Look, before I give you the go-ahead on that, let me check with the architects to make sure there aren't any structural issues to consider …

 10.3 Exam spotlight *(page 105)*

N = Narrator **P** = Presenter **D** = Dede

N Part Three. Questions 1–8.

You will hear an interview on a radio programme with Dede McGee about becoming a manager. For each question 1–8, mark one letter (A, B or C) for the correct answer. You will hear the recording twice.

P OK. In the final part of today's programme we continue our series on career progression, and this week we're taking a special look at the move from regular member of staff working alongside everyone else to becoming a manager. In the studio today we've invited Dede McGee, a freelance HR consultant, to talk to us. Dede, thanks for coming in today. What's the problem here? Presumably most people jump at the opportunity to move into management, don't they?

D Well, no. Actually, people often feel they should take a management position but they don't really ask themselves if it's really what they want.

P How do you mean?

D Well, deciding whether you want to continue working on the front line or whether you'd rather take on a management position sounds like a straightforward, logical step. But in fact it means changing how you work, how you think and the way you judge your own success. For example, do you want to be part of the team which solves big technical challenges or do you suddenly want to be the person who is in charge of encouraging others to come up with those solutions? You might find you miss being with your old colleagues. And that's another problem. New managers have to be able to tell people who were once their workmates – or equals – what to do.

P Yes, that must be a big problem.

D Well, it can work as long as you accept that your relationship with your old colleagues can never be the same. The dynamics of the relationship have to change. For example, you won't have that chance to go for a drink after work and have a quiet moan about the company any more. When you become a manager you are saying I agree with the values and direction of the company and I will work to promote these. The other big mistake, of course, is trying to please everyone all of the time. You can't. You'll have to make decisions that members of the team might not always like. You know, managers shouldn't expect love!

P No. I see. OK. But imagine we have someone who has decided management is their next career goal. What should they do?

D Funnily enough, the one thing that people don't think of doing is to go and tell their immediate boss that they want to move up.

P Is that because they're scared that their boss will think they're trying to get his or her job?

D Maybe, but in fact your manager is the first person you should talk to. They're in the best position to help by telling you what you need to do to develop. Many companies can also give you the chance to try out management roles, for example, by taking more responsibility such as mentoring new staff or taking on the duties of your boss when he or she is away. My other golden rule is to say 'yes' to any courses or training that comes your way. If there's a course on leadership or finance, take it. It'll help your professional development but also it'll be noted by the company that you're keen. It's also all part of the networking process.

P What? So you mean knowing the right people to get the promotion? Or selling yourself?

D Well, I don't think I'd be quite that cynical. Obviously, you need to let people know you are interested and – yes – selling or promoting yourself is important for promotion, as it is for that matter to get on in any part of business. But what I really mean to say is that networking with managers is also about talking to peers who can give you help and advice because as managers they face similar problems to you. Without them, management can actually be quite lonely.

P OK, so once you're a manager are there any other tips?

D I suppose one of the biggest complaints I hear from new managers is that they say 'I've been in meetings all day and haven't got any real work done'. I always have to tell them 'that's your job'. Managers delegate, they coach, they build relationships and they monitor performance. Your new role is strategic. It isn't so hands-on. The other tip I always give is that when you take over from your previous boss, listen to his or her advice but remember that you can also do things differently. You don't have to be a clone. Develop a style based on your personal strengths.

P Dede McGee. That's all we have time for now. Thanks very much for talking to us. If you'd like more information on this topic or any others in today's programme just visit our website at www. …

N Now listen to the recording again.

Module 11

 11.1 Fairtrade: an interview with Ian Bretman *(page 109)*

I = Interviewer **IB** = Ian Bretman

I So, Ian. I understand that the original idea for Fairtrade came in 1989. How did it happen?

IB Actually, the Fairtrade Foundation itself was finally set up in 1992, but yes, you're right, the catalyst for the spread of Fairtrade was three years earlier when the international coffee agreement that controlled prices collapsed with the withdrawal of the US. At that time coffee was the world's biggest agricultural commodity. In a few months the price fell by half. It was a huge disaster for the twenty million people growing and processing coffee around the world. Many of the producing countries were dependent on coffee for over half their exports.

I Can you give us some examples of how you help, exactly?

IB One way is that we encourage producers to learn how to compete effectively in international markets. We help farmers coming into the system to develop the capacity to cope with fulfilling demand and we set a minimum guaranteed price for their products.

I I see. But as well as helping farmers directly, you also have influence on governments, don't you? I mean, governments are talking more and more about fairer global trade …

IB Yes, we're finding that the issues we've been talking about for the past ten years are moving up the agenda. For example, we're having more of a debate on how we can achieve economic growth and social justice, as both are needed. As a result, leaders of larger Fairtrade organisations have been invited to high-level international meetings and economic forums. We can use our experience to illustrate to governments how trade can be better managed.

I But how do you convince people who say economic growth is the answer to everything? Don't these people argue that Fairtrade isn't good for free trade?

IB Well, I worked in business for a long time and so I understand the need for a free market, but it seems unlikely to me that when it comes to social problems, like global poverty, the answer is just an economic one, because social choices have to be made, too. Our point is really about priorities. Increasing flows of trade will help wealth but that does not necessarily guarantee that this wealth goes down to the people who need it most. That requires a little bit more management. Fairtrade has practical experience on the ground in how you can combine the best of both. How you can get people to operate effectively and competitively while trading in a way that producers can earn a decent living and improve their lives. In the long run, if they do improve their lives, they too will become consumers and purchasers.

I So is this the message you give businesses to make them change to Fairtrade products?

IB It's in the interest of any business to take the message on board, not only to improve their public image but also as a recruiting tool for the future. The younger generation is well-informed and wants to be part of the solution. Companies find that having a social conscience has a positive effect on recruiting and retaining good staff. Staff get excited about persuading consumers to buy products that make a difference to people's lives.

I It sounds like that's what motivates you, too.

IB For my part – yes – meeting the producers and seeing what a difference Fairtrade can make to their lives is really quite inspiring.

 11.2 Reasons for trends *(page 112)*

Speaker 1 I think wind power is probably a good long-term investment because its growth has been slow but fairly consistent over the last decade, and more and more wind farms seem to be appearing, so someone must be making money – unless it's all coming from government subsidies. So if you can spare some money for the next fifty years or so, I'd say you're probably on to a good thing.

Speaker 2 The whole eco-investment craze is a bit risky at this stage. It's all a bit up and down due to the fact that some governments are saying now is the time to look for alternative energies and others are still using coal and oil. It's so political that you only need a change of government and the whole thing changes again. Certainly in the short term it's going to be difficult to predict …

Speaker 3 Actually, I'd say oil is still a good one – at least in the short term. It's really kept increasing very well and I don't know anyone who's lost. Another reason for putting your money in oil companies is that quite a few are also developing environmentally-friendly fuels …

Speaker 4 It's funny, because everyone was trying to get out of nuclear energy for a while. We all thought it would be replaced with wind power and solar energy. Anyway, as a result of governments suddenly realising for at least the next century we won't be able to get enough energy from natural sources, nuclear will probably have a bit of a revival. So I wouldn't move all your money out of that industry just yet …

Speaker 5 The one you hear about least is wave power but there are one or two companies that are investing heavily in the technology. I suppose with all the sea it's worth looking into, but overall I wouldn't expect it to do well for the small, short-term investor. Anyone with money here already won't have seen much return at all and I don't predict they're going to see much change in the near future, either, as it's going to be slow to develop.

Module 12

 12.1 A colour problem *(page 116)*

P = Presenter **R** = Rene

P Business news now, and the telecoms firm Galacall has announced it may be taking legal proceedings against the newcomer and potential rival in the telecoms market, Frontline.

Frontline recently ran a series of TV commercials in which all its sales staff wore distinctive purple T-shirts. Galacall, whose trademark brand name appears in a similar shade of purple, hasn't said it will sue Frontline yet but is considering its position. Well, on the line to discuss this story is lawyer and legal expert in trademark law, Rene Mackersmann for the London-based firm Parkers and Mackersmann.

R Good morning.

P So Rene, I was wondering how serious Galacall is about all this? Surely they only have a case against a company which infringes the trademark by using a similar name, don't they?

R Well, no. In fact there are a number of examples where companies or brands have tried to prevent others from using what they consider as trademark colours. Take the case of the mobile phone company Orange trying to stop easyMobile using the colour orange. The easyGroup company had used orange on all its previous ventures, but when it launched a rival mobile phone brand, the operator Orange said easyMobile was breaking the law by using its colour in the same marketplace. Then there was the oil company BP, whose logo is green and yellow. They took out litigation against an Irish petrol company who tried to paint its petrol stations green.

P So do you think you can use the same colour as long as your product is different?

R Absolutely. For example, the food manufacturer Heinz uses turquoise on its cans but it couldn't stop someone from using the same colour on, say, bicycles.

P Can you tell me if there's anything else you can buy the rights on?

R Oh, sure. Trademarks mean firms have rights over anything like colour or shape.

P Shape as well?

R Absolutely. Take Toblerone. They have the rights on triangular boxes for their chocolate.

P So back to Galacall and Frontline. I'd like to know what you think the outcome will be if it ever gets to court. Who'll win?

R Well, I'm not the judge, but if the prosecution can prove the colour will confuse customers and damage Galacall's business then they might just win it.

P Rene Mackersmann of Parkers and Mackersmann, thank you very much.

R You're welcome.

 12.2 Difficult questions *(page 120)*

Conversation 1

S = Student   **T** = Teacher

S I'm sorry but I don't understand this mark. Why was it so low? I mean, I thought I'd answered everything. What else was I supposed to write?

T Look, I can't really comment on that until I've looked at it. Give me a day and let me get back to you on that. OK?

Conversation 2

PRM = PR Manager   **J** = Journalist

PRM OK. Are there any questions? Yes?

J So you've announced that you'll be recalling all the items from supermarkets and stores, but do you have any ideas about what caused the problem?

PRM That's a very good question. We're looking into it at the moment, and we hope that we will know more very soon.

J How soon will these items be back on the shelves?

PRM I'm afraid I'm unable to answer that at the moment. I can assure you, however, that we're doing everything we can to sort this problem out as quickly as possible.

Conversation 3

E = Employee   **M** = Manager

E Can I have a word?

M Sure.

E It's just that this doesn't seem to be right. I did some overtime the month before last. Why hasn't it been included?

M Sorry, I don't follow you. If it was for the month before last, it would have been on your last cheque.

E But don't you remember? You forgot to add it and said you'd add it to this month's …

Conversation 4

CS = Customer Service   **C** = Customer

CS Hello. Customer Service.

C Hello, I bought a Barbie doll house set and I'm afraid it's the wrong one.

CS Sorry, I didn't catch that. A Barbie what?

C A Barbie doll house set. You know. It has kind of pink wallpaper.

CS But is there something actually wrong with it?

C I think it's the wrong colour or something. I don't know really. It was my daughter who said it was wrong.

CS Well, we can only take it back if it's faulty.

C Can I exchange it for another one though?

CS Sorry. Can you wait a moment? I just need to check with someone first.

Conversation 5

M = Manager   **E** = Employee

M Sorry Peter, can I have a quick word before you go?

E Erm, well, I am in a bit of a rush.

M It won't take long. Let's use my office.

E OK.

M Take a seat. I'm aware that you've been using computers for personal use during your lunch breaks. You do know our policy with regard to this, don't you?

E Sorry, can you explain what you mean? Is there a problem?